Echoes From an Eagle

By
Ken Elder Bledsoe

COLCON
PRESS

Echoes From an Eagle

© Copyright 2016
Ken Elder Bledsoe

All rights reserved. No part of this book may be reproduced, stored in a retrieval system, or transmitted in any form or by any means, electronic, mechanical, photocopying, recording, or otherwise, without the prior written permission of the publisher.

Published by

Fort Collins, Colorado

Library of Congress Control Number: 2015918254
Printed in the United States of America
ISBN-10: 0692565124
ISBN-13: 978-0-692-56512-4

Cover & Book Design by R. Gary Raham
Copy Edited by April Moore

Introduction

It happened so fast. Gone in an instant was his smile, his laughter, all his memories and stories. Vernon Elder died in a car accident on an icy country road while on his way to work. An hour later the road was dry. Word of his death quickly spread throughout the community of his birth, La Junta, Colorado. Shock and sadness gripped those young and old who knew him. How could it be that this small town produce manager, who survived a year of intense aerial combat during World War II, died in silence on this empty road? Gone was the father his son never really knew.

Soon after his funeral my wife, Phyllis, and I began exploring his basement and discovered a small closet-sized room where he evidently spent considerable time. Its tranquil solitude must have been a calm place to pursue one of his favorite hobbies. An easel stood holding unfinished drawings and paintings, and the room had a pleasing aroma. Also in this room sat a small desk. The bottom drawer contained a tied bundle of letters along with an old scrapbook of pictures and newspaper articles. There were 46 letters, 41 penned by my father when he was stationed in California and overseas. All were addressed to my Grandmother Elder; and although he enlisted in the Army Air Corps in 1939, most of the letters dated back to the war years, specifically 1942 in Australia where he served as a tail gunner on a B-17 bomber with the 19th Bombardment Group, 30th Squadron.

After arranging them in chronological order, a dramatic experience began to unfold, revealing the most traumatic year of his life, when he flew combat missions against Japanese bases throughout the Southwest Pacific.

One article in his scrapbook always caught my attention. Faded and yellow the headline read:

"La Junta Lad Escapes Serious Injury In Pacific Plane Crash"

The article contained little information about the incident other than his bomber had crashed into the ocean, and Sgt. Houston Rice of Ordway was killed; Sgt. Elder injured; and the pilot, Lt. Paul Lindsey, of Canon City escaped injury. The three Coloradans had flown together for a long time. Rice and Elder were best friends from the same area. The three often talked about the old home state, but sadly, only one would ever see it again.

Little did Phyllis and I realize that the letters and articles written in 1942 would take us on a 10,000 mile journey 68 years after the crash, in search of their bomber that went down somewhere in the Pacific. Our goal was to find the crash site where my father's life changed forever and to bring closure to any surviving relatives of his Colorado buddies.

Echoes From an Eagle

Introduction iii
List of Maps and Photographs vii

Chapter 1   **Foundation Built on Feathers** 1
               War Drums 5
               Surprise Attack...Reverse Course 6
               Africa Route 8

Chapter 2   **Every Squeak and Rattle** 11
               First Combat 13
               Elder Evacuated 14
               'Down Under' - Regroup, Reload, Retaliate . 17
               'Bush' Base - Cloncurry 19
               Battle of the Coral Sea 23

Chapter 3   **"Somewhere, Someplace, Overseas"** 25
               "It's either your life or theirs" 25
               19th Bombing Missions-
                  A logistical nightmare 26
               19th Bomb Group: Predominant
                  Areas of Operation - 1942 28
               Horn Island 28
               Marooned 30

Chapter 4   **Mareeba** 31
               Target: Rabaul 33
               Scenes at Mareeba 35
               Letters home 37

Chapter 5   **Wounded Eagle** 41
               "Guess we tried to be a submarine" 41
               The Crew of #655, "Hitching a ride"
                  Sgt. Edward 'Ralph' Dietz 43
               Other Costly Crashes on Horn Island 52
               Great Raid on Rabaul Aug. 7, 1942 53

	Flare Test Tragedy 55
	"From one anxious mother to another" 59
	Coming Home 61
Chapter 6	**'Rattlesnake' Bomber Base 1943-45** 67
	Last Mission 71
	Unfinished Business 72
	Buffalo Hide Calendar..73
	Moving on 76
Chapter 7	**Australian Connection** 81
	Seekee and Dietz..81
	In Their Steps 83
Chapter 8	**'The Letter'** 85
	The Letter Exchange 87
	"He was my closest friend"..................................89
Chapter 9	**Adventure 'Down Under'** 95
	In his steps at Mareeba Air Base 96
	Ngurapai, (Horn Island) 100
	The Torres Strait Islanders 103
	Sarpeye: A Dinner to Remember....................105
Chapter 10	**Long Ago But Not Forgotten** 109
	Echoes from the past 114
Summary..115
Epilogue	**The Cappelletti-Lindsey Connection**
	Lindsey Reunion-2012 117
Echoes From an Eagle 121
Bibliography 123
Notes and References..134
Acknowledgements 139

List of Maps and Photographs

Cover
Sgt. Vernon Elder standing by his B-17 tail gun.
Mareeba, Queensland, Australia, 1942

Vernon in dress uniform x

Chapter 1
Eagle Dance costume 4
Senior Picture 1936..4
Three Amigos...6
Africa Route...9
Western Union telegram...10

Chapter 2
Scenes from S.E. Asia: Java...11
S.W. Pacific Theater..12
Western Union telegram...14
19th BG squadron assignments..19
Scenes from Cloncurry 20
Local attractions...21

Chapter 3
Southwest Pacific battleground..27
Torres Strait — Horn Island..28
Horn Island landing field 29
B-17s taking off from Horn Island...29

Chapter 4
Landing at Mareeba 31
Port Moresby, New Guinea..32
New Guinea 33
Scenes at Mareeba... 35-36
B-17 Preparing for mission/On the way to a target 36
Scenes at Mareeba Airfield 38-40

vii

List of Maps and Photographs

Chapter 5
Sgt. Houston Rice, 30th BS 42
Lt. Paul Lindsey, 30th BS 43
2nd Lt. Robert M. Kernan 44
2nd Lt. Edward R. Budz 44
S/Sgt. James E. Houchins 44
Sgt. Edward (Ralph) Dietz 45
Ralph Dietz and 93rd crewmates 46
Sgt. Rice shortly before his crash 47
Australian crash boat..48
Vernon in 'woolies' 49
Sgt. Vernon Elder by his B-17 tail gun 49
Sgt. Buller 50
Elder and Buller with friends...50
Paul Lindsey in flight training...56
Paul Lindsey at Colorado A&M 57
Sgt. Vernon Elder's watch 58
Gen. Kenney presenting medals 58
USTS Torrens 62
Coming home...62
Returning from Australia 63
Entering San Francisco Bay...63
19th BG Officers, Mareeba, 1942...65
B-17 #636 wreckage 66
Map of crash sites off Horn Island..66

Chapter 6
"Beware Rattlesnakes"..67
Public relations picture, Pyote Air Base 68
Vernon receiving 'Air Medal' 69
First home in Monahans...69
Vernon, Mom, and T.J. Rice...69
Buffalo Hide Calendar 73
Vernon & Ken near Raton, NM 79
Grandmother Elder & Mildred, Vernon's sister..............................79

List of Maps and Photographs

Family photo 80
Vanessa Seekee 80
Author, Vanessa Seekee, and Phyl 80

Chapter 7
Dietz returns to Australia 83
A visit with Ralph Dietz..84

Chapter 9
Scenes at Mareeba.. 97-98
Kaurareg Aboriginal Nation...99
Slit trench in the 'bush'..101
Croc warnings 102
Beer bottles from 1943..102
Plane wreckage 102
C Company, FNQR, Royal Australian Army................104
Morris Nona from Badu Island....................................104
RAA vets singing Thursday Island Song 105
Dedication at bunker...107
Gordon Cameron and Ken 107
Gerry Merrett and Ken..108
Major Mark Prideaux, RAA..108

Chapter 10
Eddie, the optimist 110
Liberty and me searching for 655 110
Sam spotting the location..111
Anchor chain over wreckage 111
Part of engine and wreckage 112
Catching a breath 112
Flag from Vernon's grave..112
Phyl 113

Epilogue
Lt. Frank Cappelletti 118
Lindsey Reunion—2012 119

Echoes From an Eagle

1
CHAPTER

Foundation Built on Feathers

Working as a painter for the Santa Fe Railroad, Albert Elder, was the only source of income for his wife, Lerenna, and their four children, my father, Vernon, being the youngest. When the great flu epidemic of 1919 took Albert's life, the family did not have to wait for the Depression to experience economic hardship. Lerenna, the diminutive head of house, never remarried and took whatever jobs were available to support, as best she could, her children. By cooking at a boarding house and working in a small department store, Lerenna provided the family's basic needs. When she got off work at 9:00 p.m., young Vernon and his older sister, Mildred, would often meet their tired mother and walk her home. Occasionally, the family could splurge and go to the Saturday movies where admission cost 10 cents each. This was one of the few types of entertainment the family could afford during these hard times.

"It takes a village to raise a child," certainly held true in the small, southeastern Colorado town of La Junta. The Elders lived on the edge of town and neighbored a farm family. The two households worked out a barter system where the Elders would get food in exchange for house cleaning, and young Vernon did 'boy chores' around the yard and barns. Other neighbors took the family into town and bought the children clothes for school. None of this was considered charity, but instead came from the belief that everyone worked together and helped each other through life's challenges.

Young Vernon was held in his father's arms for only a year. The man who did much to fill this vacuum in Vernon's life, and set his moral compass, was 'Buck' Burshears. Having been positively influenced by scouting in the Arkansas Valley during the 1920s, Buck saw the need to provide a program for the boys in La Junta. Therefore, he organized a group that not only included the outdoor activities of the Boy Scouts but also incorporated an extensive study of the Indians who once roamed southeastern Colorado. This troop became known as the Koshare Indians. The initial group of seven or eight boys, Vernon being one of them, learned the dances of the American Plains Indians. The young scouts then made authentic costumes and began presenting dance programs for local audiences. As their village chief, Buck instilled in these young men a love of art, music, and history. He also taught them the rewards of investing in something greater than themselves, emphasizing the values of duty, honor, and country.[1]

    The time with Buck filled a huge void in the development of my father's young life. The lessons learned in the Koshare troop prepared him for challenges he would soon face. Featured in the Koshare dance program was the Eagle Dance performed by Vernon on the famous 'Thunder Drum.' This dance depicted an eagle caught in a trap. It is said Vernon showed excellent understanding of the pantomime, with the great wings he carried circling ever nearer the imaginary trap until with a scream he was caught. How prophetic the dance would become years later.

    I didn't know my father very well. He and my mother met before his assignment overseas and married after his return from a year of combat in the Southwest Pacific. They divorced several years later, not an uncommon consequence when long dangerous deployments interrupted courtships.

    After the war, Vernon started a small grocery store down the street from Grandmother's house. Every day at lunch hour, with his apron tucked over his belt, he walked the few blocks from his store to Grandmother's. As he neared, he'd whistle, signaling his approach, and I'd run out of the house to meet him. He always brought me a little toy that probably came from a cereal

Chapter 1: Foundation Built on Feathers

box or one of his vendors. Airplanes were my favorite, and I provided the background sounds.

Vernon was born and raised in La Junta, and seemed to be known and respected by everyone. Everywhere we went people smiled, laughed, and had long conversations with him. They called him 'Skeets' and me 'Skeeter.' Occasionally, he brought out a box containing a model he had made of a B-17 'Flying Fortress.' Painted a dark olive green, it had decals with rows of black bombs on one side of the fuselage and a row of Japanese 'rising sun' flags on the other side. A logo of a 'policeman' was painted on both sides of the cockpit, which I later learned was a squadron insignia. He'd let me play with it for short periods of time before putting it back in the box. A few years later, he gave me the bomber to keep, not realizing that decades later I would be searching for a bigger version.

Mom remarried, and at age ten I was adopted. By court order, my last name changed from Elder to Bledsoe. My stepfather's background in aviation enhanced my own interest in the field. I still went to visit Vernon occasionally, but he often seemed tired, nervous, and melancholy. However, we were always glad to see each other and to catch up on our separate lives. He never talked about his past, and I never asked.

Then as fate would have it, his untimely death in a car accident just two weeks prior to meeting my wife, Phyllis, forever ended any chance of my hearing his stories. I intended to explore the letters, pictures, and scrapbooks we brought home with us to discover more about Vernon's experiences during a traumatic year of his life. However, my own life was dominated by career changes, moves, and raising a family, so Vernon's story lay dormant in my closet for many years.

After my retirement, I finally set out to learn as much as possible about Vernon's year overseas as the tail gunner on a B-17. I began my search by reading his collection of letters. Generally, in the early part of 1942, letters took about two months to reach their destination. Some were interrupted by the necessity of last minute bombing missions, and all had been opened and censored by the military. Vernon's letters covered the period from a month before the attack on Pearl Harbor to his return stateside in December of 1942, just over a complete year.

Ironically, by embarking on this undertaking, I came to know my father through his correspondence with my grandmother and aunt. I learned of his unwavering patriotism, optimism, devotion to duty, and dedication to his fellow airmen.

He continued to reassure his family by encouraging them to go on with their lives. He consistently sent most of his pay to his mother and encouraged her to take a vacation. In reading his letters one can sense the subtle changes in his attitude and detect the strain on him both physically and mentally. In two of his letters he admitted becoming very nervous and that he might have to quit flying for a while. He had flown over forty combat missions. In one letter he tells his mother, "I know I've done my share of flying so far and have had enough thrills and excitement to do me the rest of my life."[2]

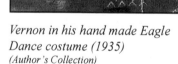

Vernon in his hand made Eagle Dance costume (1935)
(Author's Collection)

Senior Picture (1936)
(Author's Collection)

Chapter 1: Foundation Built on Feathers

War Drums

Growing up in southeast Colorado during the 1930s was especially difficult. Vernon graduated from La Junta High School in1937. The economy throughout this part of the country relied on agriculture, cattle, and the railroad. The economic consequences of the Great Depression, along with the horrific effects of the dust bowl throughout eastern Colorado and western Kansas, forced many young men and women to seek opportunity and jobs far from their hometowns. For many, this meant the military.

Influenced by lessons learned in the Koshares that stressed loyalty, responsibility, and sacrifice, Vernon enlisted in the Army Air Corps in 1939, just shy of his 22nd birthday. He trained primarily in aircraft armament (bombardment and gunnery) at Lowry Field in Denver, March Field in California, and Kirtland Field in Albuquerque. With him were his best friends, Houston Rice of Ordway, Colorado and T.J. Rice from Washington. The three hung around together during their training in California and Albuquerque.

By 1941, Vernon was assigned to the 19th Bomb Group at Fort McDowell, California. The 19th Bomb Group gradually grew to include the 14th, 30th, 32nd and 93rd Squadrons, as well as, the 32nd Reconnaissance. Authorized by the War Department, the bomb group's motto was: In Alis Vicimus: 'On Wings We Conquer.'[3]

In early October of 1941, the 19th BG ground echelons sailed from San Francisco destined for Manila, Philippines. Later the 14th Squadron departed to ferry twenty-six B-17E Flying Fortress bombers across the Pacific to the Philippines. In early November, all but one Fortress had arrived at Clark Field.

Vernon, Houston, and T.J. arrived at Fort McDowell in late November. Vernon and Houston were in the 30th Squadron while T.J. flew in the 93rd. They all served as crew members on the Flying Fortresses. These 'three amigos' had no way of knowing the hair-raising experiences they would soon share. Beyond the shores of the U.S., rising powers in Europe and Asia brought about a national challenge that forever defined these young men. Whatever aspirations they had, would end or be delayed during the first half of the coming decade.

"At a time in their lives when their days and nights should have been filled with innocent adventure, love, and lessons of the workday world, they were fighting often hand to hand in the most primitive conditions possible, across the bloodied landscape of France, Belgium, Italy, and Austria. They fought their way up a necklace of South Pacific Islands few had ever heard of before and made them a fixed part of American History - islands with names like Iwo Jima, Guadalcanal, Okinawa. They were in the air every day in skies filled with terror and they went to sea on hostile waters far removed from the shores of their homeland."[4]

*The 'three amigos"
T.J., Houston, Vernon*

Surprise Attack...Reverse Course

With their final destination and departure date uncertain, Vernon and other crewmen in the air echelon of his squadron were ordered to board the *SS President Johnson* destined for Pearl Harbor. His letters written from Fort McDowell or in the dark aboard ship, reflected his boredom, frustration, and anxiety.[5]

Chapter 1: Foundation Built on Feathers

November 28, 1941	"anxious to sail to Pearl Harbor; tired of waiting"
December 3, 1941	"anxious to get mail; date to set sail for Hawaii"
December 4, 1941	"sailing tomorrow, arriving eventually in Philippines"
December 6, 1941	"pretty rough, fellows getting sick, packed in like cattle; two meals a day"
December 7, 1941	"heard Japs bombed Pearl Harbor; we turned around and headed back the way we came; heard report our ship is missing and been sunk. Life boat drills, must wear life vests, ship blacked out, full steam ahead. Fellows trying to cheer themselves up with singing and playing guitars." (about 700 miles out)
December 8, 1941	"they had this crate going as fast as it would go. Still blacked out, patrol bombers flying overhead, good feeling."

Coinciding with the attack on Pearl Harbor (the morning of December 8, Philippine Island time), the Japanese attacked Clark Field in the Philippines. The only warning was a low whistling noise, followed quickly by a deafening crash, and then explosion after explosion. Some of those out on the field had seen the formation of 54 Japanese bombers in time to jump into slit trenches. Others did not and were blasted from the earth as they stood by their airplanes.

The entire attack lasted 40 minutes. The casualties were heavy, and Clark Field was a wreck. Of the 19 Flying Fortresses there, 12 were completely destroyed and five more damaged . . .

two were flying and escaped the disaster. Supplies and headquarters were hastily moved from Clark Field to comparatively safe points nearby. Planes not heavily damaged were given emergency repairs and dispatched to Del Monte in Mindanao. For the next 10 days the surviving Fortresses, now based at Del Monte, participated in valiant but futile bombing attacks against the Japanese invasion swarming ashore on Luzon.

On January 1, 1942 the remaining flyable B-17s of the 19th were sent to Java to assist in the defense of the Dutch East Indies. Personnel from the 19th Bomb Group escaping from the Philippines merged with those of the 7th BG in Java.[6]

Meanwhile, after arriving safely back in San Francisco, Vernon and other members of the 19th BG, camped in a park in pup tents. Though damp and cold, they were glad to have made it back to port safely. Once again, these men had no way of knowing what lay ahead and could only wait for their new orders. Vernon's letters revealed some impatience and a sense of uncertainty in what was about to happen.[7]

December 11, 1941	"Sure hope we can move out soon though can't win a war sitting here."
December 22, 1941	"I have been assigned bombardier on new B-17E (Flying Fortress), we are leaving tomorrow morning... first stop will be Tampa... going somewhere but don't know... we have a 12,000 mile trip by air... must be going a long ways."

Africa Route

With the Pacific route blocked by the Japanese Navy, the new B-17Es had to be ferried via the 'Africa Route' to bases in the

Chapter 1: Foundation Built on Feathers

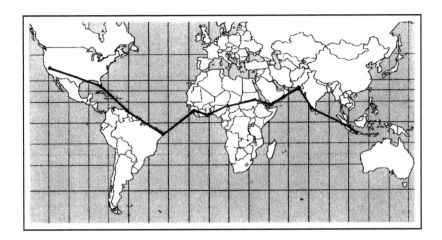

Dutch East Indies and the Philippines. Vernon and his squadron departed from Bakersfield, California on December 23, 1941. On his journey to the Dutch East Indies, this small-town boy from southeastern Colorado, experienced parts of the world he'd never imagined seeing: Brazil, Africa's Sahara Desert, Southwest Asia, and India. Most of the flights between bases were long; and in one case, Vernon's bomber got lost over the Sahara Desert and finally returned to base after 13 hours of flying. In another segment of the route, Vernon's plane blew a tire and collapsed the retracting motor mount stranding them for a few days. After landing in Khartoum, the crew received cholera shots and then visited some of the sights. At this point, Vernon's letters started to reflect some homesickness.[8]

". . . all our letters are now censored . . . interesting but tell all my friends at home that I rather miss the good old U.S. after seeing a few of these places." Jan. 4, 1942.

". . . give ten dollars for a letter from home . . . Many different people but this African Arab lingo is about to get me down. We visited an old Arab city yesterday . . . it was interesting but they can have my share of them." Jan. 14, 1942.

Echoes From an Eagle

Nearly four weeks following their departure from Bakersfield, California and logging over 12,000 miles of flying through severe equatorial tropical storms, blistering Saharan dust storms, and getting lost, Vernon writes on January 21:

_____, India

"The last letter I wrote you was in_____we are still not certain where we are going but its quite possible it will be _____. I've seen a lot of things on this trip that I never knew existed."

<u>NOTE</u>: *His letter was censored. He most likely wrote it from Bangalore, India, location of a British airbase.*

The last leg of his 'Africa Route' took the longest, over 12 hours from Bangalore to Palembang, Sumatra finally arriving in Malang, Java on January 23rd. The situation in Java was deteriorating, and within hours of arriving, Vernon sent the following telegram to his mother perhaps thinking it would be his last message.[9]

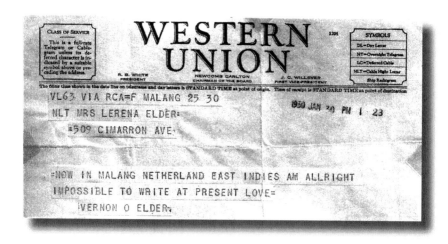

2
CHAPTER

Every Squeak and Rattle

If the new air crews had any advantage, it was gained through their long and arduous journey half way around the world. They knew their bomber inside and out . . . every 'squeak and rattle,' and they worked together to maximize their effectiveness, but the ultimate test of men and machine in combat, was soon to come.

Meanwhile in the Philippines, twenty-two B-17s had been destroyed in three weeks of war, and despite the valiant efforts of the air and ground crews, the powerful Japanese forces rapidly moved south, making air operations on Mindanao increasingly difficult. The field at Del Monte had been bombed on several occasions, strafed by Japanese fighters almost daily. Bombing strikes by the 19th Bomb Group had

Scenes from Java (Author's collection)

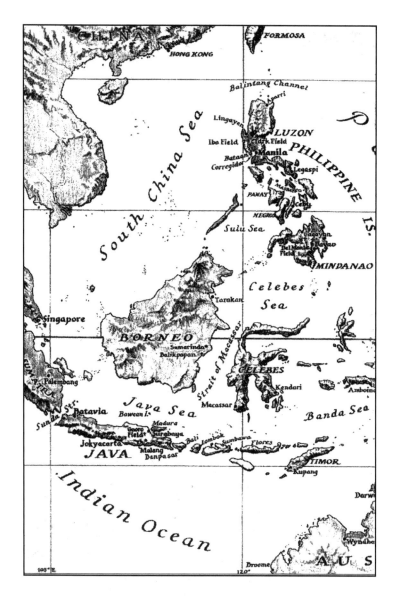

proven mostly ineffective in stemming the Japanese invasion; thus, by the middle of January, Java-based 17s, including many from the 19th BG, began evacuating personnel from Mindanao. The planes arrived at dusk, and during the night passengers were loaded. The planes then took off for Java before dawn. To save

Chapter 2: Every Squeak and Rattle

the surviving B-17s from air attack at Del Monte, officials relocated them 1500 miles away at Batchelor Field near Darwin, Australia.

At the end of 1941, the 19th received orders to fly to Java. They were to help defend the Dutch East Indies—the next Japanese objective in their strategy to conquer all of the SW Pacific.

First Combat

Pfc. Vernon Elder arrived in Java as one of the air crew on B-17 #41-2455 under the command of 1st Lt. P. L. Mathewson. Within hours, Vernon flew his first combat mission as tail gunner attacking Japanese transports at Balikpanpan, located on the eastern coast of Borneo.[1] For nearly a month, he flew missions over Borneo, the Celebes, Timor, and Bali against overwhelming odds and a Japanese air force that proved far better than anticipated. All too often, thick tropical clouds shrouded the targets; and severe thunderstorms made it necessary for the bombers to attempt their runs at low altitudes, making the planes vulnerable to antiaircraft fire. For most of the missions during the next four weeks, Vernon's crew on #2455 were the same guys he flew with on the 'Africa Route.'

Vernon's small stature was a determining factor for his assignment as a tail gunner.

> "It was lonely, cramped, and you assumed a kneeling position. In rough air tail gunners needed to have a strong resistance to airsickness. There wasn't much room to move around, only enough space to put a pair of gun barrels, if you had them, and a couple of boxes of ammunition and a parachute. On the right side of the aircraft there was a small escape door to be used in the event of an emergency. Enemy fighters would take bold chances to put the tail gunner out of action."[2]

Elder Evacuated

In the closing days of February, 1942, the remaining battered fortresses manned by crews of the 30th Squadron and others from the 19th Group, completed at least four evacuation missions from Java before operations ceased. On these final missions from Java, the Group's B-17s, which in peace time would have been considered unserviceable, carried at least 25 to 30 passengers through severe tropical storms to Perth, Australia via Darwin and Broome.

Feb. 26, 1942—To Australia. The following crews and passengers departed Malang 0145 for South Base. All passengers to remain there, crews to return tonight.[3]

No. 2453	No. 2497	Passengers	Passengers	Passengers	Passengers
P Teats	Key, FM	Maj McDonald	Lt Heald	Sgt Strahecker	Pvt Guth
CP Beekman	Holdridge	Capt. McDonald	Lt Norvell	Sgt Whitehead	Pvt French
N Hoffman	Tarbutton	Capt.Montgomery	Lt O'Bryan	Sgt May	
E Clark	Baca	Capt. Cummins	Lt Gregg	**Pfc Elder**	
R Norgaard	Shafer	Lt. Jacques	Sgt Payne	Pfc Bernardzya	
G Colburn	Chytel	Lt. Cobb	Sgt Peterson	Pfc Crabtree	
G Billen	French	Lt. Stripling	Sgt Randell	Pfc Michelson	

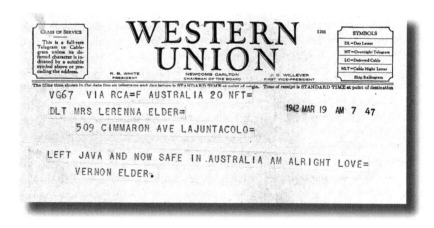

Chapter 2: Every Squeak and Rattle

Vernon was fortunate to get out of Java early. Perhaps being an experienced tail gunner with 10 missions to his credit made him too valuable to leave. He flew to Broome then on to Sydney with fellow Coloradan and pilot, Lt. Paul Lindsey, of Canon City. From Sydney, Lt. Lindsey and Vernon flew back to Melbourne.

Vernon's other buddies, Sgt. Houston Rice and Pfc. T. J. Rice (no relation), also evacuated to Australia. Only a handful of Air Corps personnel got out. Bataan became the end of the road for the great majority. Of the 210 officers, 70 were left behind; of the 1300 enlisted men, 1060 were either killed or captured and imprisoned in the Philippines. Americans who went into the hills and jungles rather than surrender were known as AGOM (American Guerillas of Mindanao). Half of them had been in the 19th Bomb Group. They had nothing but praise for the Philippine people, without whose help they would not have survived.[4]

As the situation in Java deteriorated, the 19th and 7th Bomb Groups began evacuating the airfields. In anticipation of this evacuation, a 12,000 ton Dutch freighter, *Abbekerk*, was pre-positioned at Tjilaljap, Java. Long lines of American, Dutch, Javanese, English, and Australians crammed on board, including hundreds of military personnel. Finally, on February 27th, the over-packed *Abbekerk* departed for Fremantle, Australia with 1700 refugees. The voyage endured a Japanese bomber attack and the fears of being torpedoed. Adverse weather conditions made sleeping on the deck difficult. After four anxious days and nights, the Australian coast came within sight, and the vessel finally sailed safely into Fremantle, docking the same afternoon.

"In total, several thousand Allied Air Force personnel were successfully evacuated by air and sea from Java under the nose of the invading Japanese. However, thousands more Allied servicemen fell into the hands of an enemy not noted for his compassionate treatment of POWs. The costly Java campaign was recognized as a frustrating failure which achieved little. A mood of despondency followed in the wake of the debacle."[5]

By March 1st when it became evident the East Indies would be conquered by the Japanese, the surviving U. S. planes and crews were evacuated to Australia. The Dutch flew hundreds of men, women, and children to Broome, easily doubling its population. Since Broome was within range of the Japanese, the Aussies quickly provided transportation to a safer location further south at Perth. Indeed, on March 3rd the Japanese attacked Broome and shot down a departing B-24, killing 33. The attack left 33 additional airmen and 45 civilians dead, and destroyed 22 planes.

Fearful of another raid, the 5th Bomber Command ordered the relocation of Americans south to Perth. After 10 days of R& R, the personnel of the 19th Bomb Group loaded onto troop trains destined for Melbourne. Houston Rice, one of the 'three amigos' was among them. At most stops, patriotic ladies waited on the railroad platforms beside long tables heaped with sandwiches, cake and other goodies. When crossing from one Australian state to another, the gauge of tracks would be different necessitating the transfer of troops to a different train.

No communication came from Vernon for the next three months because,

> "On March 1, the USAAFFE (United States Armed Forces in the Far East) banned all under its command from mentioning in private correspondence any references to the effect of Japanese operations, casualties suffered or equipment destroyed in advance of any official announcements on the subject."[6]

Chapter 2: Every Squeak and Rattle

'Down Under' – Regroup, Reload, Retaliate

Forced to fight a predominately defensive holding action throughout the Philippines and Java, the 19th Bomb Group moved to Melbourne in early March of 1942. A tremendous toll had been taken on the men and planes. Weary crews needed rest and recuperation; planes needed repair and parts. Upon arrival in Melbourne, the troops had no formal reception, but the Australian people made sure they were not neglected.

> "Probably nowhere in the world have troops received as warm a welcome as did ours from the hospitable Australians. Everything a soldier fresh from combat could want was theirs for the asking, and they did not need to ask. For two weeks they enjoyed the lights and parties provided by the people of Melbourne. Military organization and discipline became loose . . . the situation was so bad that three quarters of the officers might fail to attend a squadron meeting."[7]

Despite the warm reception, however, the pain and loss suffered during combat, weighed heavily on the servicemen.

> "Morale was low; they were tired and their planes were worn and abused beyond limits . . .The men of the shattered 19th and remnants of 7th Group, dispirited, fatigued and without hope, could not help but wonder what was in store for them next. Painfully and at great cost and for what appeared to be minimal results, they had heroically made it up as they went along."[8]

Americans had been heartened by the 'Doolittle raids' on Japan, yet events in Europe overshadowed the courageous efforts of our troops and flyers in the SW Pacific. The men of the 19th considered themselves losers and abandoned—lacking any support from America. Many of the most experienced pilots had gone to India with the 7th Group. The men considered themselves lucky to have gotten out of Java to the safety of Australia, for a much deserved break.[9]

Many men who showed no outward physical disabilities, nonetheless, suffered 'shell shock' or other psychological disturbances from their war experiences. Some of these problems became long lasting.[10]

Not enough active personnel survived from the 19th or the component of the 7th Bombardment Group which reached Australia, to form even one composite group. Army Air Force personnel from other U.S. units substituted into the new 19th Group to bring it to full strength. Royal Australian Air Force navigators were employed to make up a shortage of trained aircrews.[11]

On March 12, 1942, after two weeks of R&R, headquarters of the 19th Bomb Group in Melbourne issued a directive. The 19th was to be reorganized to include the 14th Reconnaissance, the 30th, 28th, 93rd, and 435th (Kangaroo) Bomb Squadrons. Effort went into placing their bases in interior areas of sparsely populated Queensland far from the reach of a Japanese attack. They would operate against targets to the northeast of Australia in the New Guinea and New Britain areas. On April 18th, two months after its evacuation from Java, the refurbished 19th BG was ready to move from Melbourne. By that time, the enemy had firmly established itself in northern New Guinea with forces threatening Port Moresby.[12]

Only one Allied Bomber Group had the weight and range to maintain this sphere of defense by attacking Japanese bases beyond Australia—the B-17 equipped 19th. Crews were assigned to planes and squadrons and given orders to proceed to the following locations: 30th BS to Cloncurry (Vernon, Houston Rice, and Paul Lindsey here); 28th and 93rd to Longreach (T.J. Rice here); 14th and 435th (Kangaroo) to Townsville.

Chapter 2: Every Squeak and Rattle

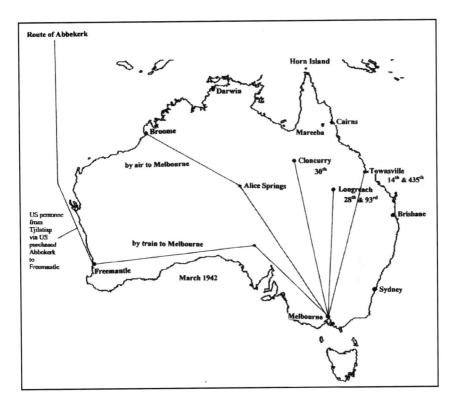

'Bush' Base – Cloncurry

The 30th Bomb Squadron first operated out of Cloncurry, as did initially, the 93rd Squadron. Located about 500 miles west of Townsville on the edge of the great Australian outback, the landscape resembled scenes from old western movies with dirt streets and one hotel. Rain came only one month a year, and mosquitoes outnumbered the flies two to one. The airfield was outside of town, among dried-up stream beds, with a few trees occupied by cockatoo birds. "To the locals, these big B-17s looked like awesome machines from another world as they watched them roar down the oil-soaked runway on their way to Japanese targets."[13]

Instead of the Japanese fighter planes that had plagued the men in Java, mosquitoes seemed to be the big problem at Cloncurry:

"At night if you wanted a good night's sleep, a mosquito bar [holding aloft a mosquito net] was necessary; and if your bare body came in contact with the netting, you had a big red spot with an infection coming if you did not medicate it ... It was always a good habit to wear boots all the time . . .I almost got nailed by a six foot cobra."[14]

The animals also provided both frustration and amusement, as is evidenced by this quote:

"There was an interesting collection of livestock here. There were large groves of eucalyptus trees on either side of the runway where a large group of kangaroos dwelled. Every so often they'd get the urge to visit the grove on the other side and would take their time about it, frequently stopping to play around (horse around?) in the middle of the runway. If an airplane was about to take off during this performance, it was necessary to send out a truck filled with people shooting .45's in the air to shoo them back into the woods. Sometimes they didn't shoo worth a damn, so here was a truck full of G.I.s careening around uncooperative kangaroos, and a pilot sitting at the end of the runway with his engine heating up and cursing anything and everything that had to do with Australia." [15]

Cloncurry (R.B. Gooch)

Chapter 2: Every Squeak and Rattle

General Douglas MacArthur, commander of the American forces in the Philippines, was flown out and relocated to Australia. He intended to defend Australia by striking the growing Japanese forces located along the north coast of New Guinea as well as New Britain.

Japan gained control of Rabaul, and it became their mightiest base in the SW Pacific. Surrounded by volcanoes that provided a natural barrier and a deep harbor for the largest of war ships, Rabaul was virtually impenetrable from attack. Using trucks, horses, native laborers and prisoners, Japan developed Rabaul into the most heavily fortified stronghold south of the equator. With Rabaul as the center of operations, the enemy could now expand their domination over the entire South Pacific from the Solomon Islands to New Guinea.[16]

Local Attractions—
(Author's collection)

But recognizing its strategic importance, the American Command began air operations at once to hinder the Japanese build-up. Because Rabaul proved to be a difficult target, the crews dreaded going there. Missions would begin from the outback bases and Townsville and would then refuel and load bombs at Horn Island off the northern tip of Cape York or Port Moresby in New Guinea. These forward locations were vital to both the Australians and Americans. Should the Japanese take Port Moresby, they would not only be able to shut down a major Allied base but would themselves have a jumping-off place for their proposed Australian campaign.[17]

The 19th BG continued to be based at small, out of the way places, far from any large Australian city and its diversions.

The constantly changing facilities, the lack of recreation, and even the unfamiliarity with the Australian food and drink, played havoc with the fragile morale. Additionally, it became difficult to maintain their battered B-17s on a supply line that stretched 7500 miles back to the United States. A shortage of spare parts and trained mechanics, along with bad landing fields, ever-changing weather, long missions, and unending combat left only 50 percent of the airplanes ready at any given time.[18] During the month of April, consistently bad weather hampered the missions against the Japanese. Flying at only 9000 feet, B-17 #2505, slammed into the north side of Mt. Obree in the Owen Stanley Mountains of New Guinea killing the entire eight-man crew. Yet, in spite of these hardships, the 19th BG continued to function. By the end of the month, the arrival of new B-17s from the United States brought the total number of 'Fortresses' in Australia to 40.

From Cloncurry, Vernon's 30th Squadron found they could bomb Lae or Salamaua on the northwest coast of New Guinea and even Rabaul by flying from RAAF forward bases, but these were also becoming unsafe.

Missions from Cloncurry normally staged out of Horn Island or Port Moresby, thus, adding striking range for the bombers. These locales also allowed crews to modify the bomb loads when they had a change of target. In addition, the available facilities on these forward bases made it possible for the crews to get the rest needed to fly another mission the following day.

But the trying conditions and poor facilities in central Queensland, which the Americans had made the best of, were not just a nuisance. One pilot, Lt. "Spoon" Sponable, remembered:

> "The flies were a problem but not really a major problem once we got used to them. Our major operating problem was dusty operating conditions; and as a result, we got very poor engine-life and had many maintenance problems due to

Chapter 2: Every Squeak and Rattle

those dusty conditions. The initial reason for us basing our Squadron at Cloncurry, so far inland, was that the future of Darwin and in fact the entire northern part of the Australian continent was, at that time, in considerable jeopardy. So we were really there in case the Japanese did make an invasion. As it happened, our principal targets were to remain in New Guinea and New Britain."[19]

Battle of the Coral Sea: May 3-8, 1942

As predicted by the Allied commanders, the Japanese fleet intended to capture Port Moresby and Midway Island, thus, establishing a staging area for their attack on Melanesia and Australia. When the Japanese launched their Port Moresby Invasion Force, the Pacific Fleet and their Allies planned to intercept them in the Coral Sea.[20]

B-17s from the 19th Group and B-26s from the 22nd Group were alerted for reconnaissance and bombardment.[21] As fate would have it, Vernon took part in this battle, flying tail gunner in one of three B-17s from the 30th Bomb Squadron based in Cloncurry. On May 6th, Capt. Harlow, Lt. Beasley, and Lt. Spieth of the 435th Squadron spotted the carrier *Shoho* and proceeded to bomb it. Lt. Rouse of the 93rd Squadron said later they should have bombed in formation because it was impossible to hit a maneuvering ship with one aircraft. Though the B-17s inflicted no damage, the Japanese task force had been sighted. The B-17 crews reported their sightings allowing the American carrier force to adjust course.

The Battle of the Coral Sea was the first naval battle in history where opposing ships never came in sight of one another. The entire action was fought by carrier-borne aircraft.[22] Following the coordinates reported by the B-17 crews, Navy dive bombers and torpedo planes from the U.S. carriers *Yorktown* and *Lexington* sank the Japanese carrier *Shoho* . . . A furious counter attack by Japanese aircraft, however, so badly damaged the *Lexington* that it was eventually sunk by an American destroyer. Two other Japanese carriers sustained heavy damage, putting them out of action for two months.[23]

Both the Japanese Invasion Force and the U.S. Pacific Fleet experienced so many mistakes during the Coral Sea battle that the servicemen began to view them with 'grim humor.' For example, three B-17s from Townsville dropped bombs in the vicinity of *HMAS Australia*, *USS Faragut*, and *USS Perkins*, mistaking them for Japanese. Thankfully, their bombardiers had poor aim, and no damage was done. Six Japanese fighter pilots, on the other hand, tried to land on *Yorktown*, thinking she was a Japanese carrier.[24] Not a good decision for them.

Although there were major mistakes and losses suffered by the Allied Forces, strategically, they were victorious. Due to the lack of adequate air cover, the Port Moresby Invasion Force retreated.[25] The Allies had stopped a Japanese invasion armada for the first time since Pearl Harbor. Therefore, the Battle of the Coral Sea proved to be an indispensable preliminary action that contributed to the victory at Midway.

After the Coral Sea battle, co-pilots of all crews became first pilots and took the place of the older pilots who went to staff positions in and outside the squadrons. Replacements came including Australians, to serve as co-pilots. The Aussies were readily accepted in all the squadrons and proved to be efficient crew men.

3
CHAPTER

Somewhere, Someplace, Overseas

The first letter from Australia Vernon's family received was written on May 22, 1942. In it he acknowledged receiving his first mail from home, which clearly boosted his morale. His family consisted of his mother, two older sisters, and an older brother. He continued to insist that his mother deposit his monthly pay and treat herself to a vacation and said his pay would increase since all combat gunners were being promoted to sergeant. What follows is an excerpt from his letter:

"It's either your life or theirs"

Letter written home by Vernon, May 22, 1942 from Cloncurry:

> "We really have had a lot of exciting experiences and not all of them pleasant but you have to expect those kind of things while there is a war. We're all doing our best over here and naturally we all look forward to the time we can get back home. Probably a lot of boys are anxious to get over here and have a crack at the Japs but all I can say is that they don't realize just what they are getting into and what you have to go through at times. I'm still on combat duty and have seen a lot of action and it's still hard for me to realize that when you're up in the air fighting it's either your life or theirs and they're not about to get me yet."[1]

19th Bombing Missions - A logistical nightmare

From mid-March through June of 1942 the squadrons were extremely limited in equipment. More often than not, no more than six bombers could be sent on a mission from a single squadron. In addition to this was the notable strain combat had on the personnel.

> "A number of our men were beginning to be burned out as well as suffering from the effects of Dengue fever, a mosquito borne disease which would smack a man down for weeks. He aches all over. Food . . . even good food has no attraction at all. Plenty of the fellows were on the ragged edge, but they kept going. It wasn't heroism. There was a job to do, and not anywhere near enough equipment and men to do it."[2]

During the first three weeks of June, the Group conducted 14 missions, 11 of which took place on Rabaul and the nearby Vunakanau airdrome. Bombers also continued to attack Lae and Salamaua on the northern coast of New Guinea.

All these missions were divided into two hops. Because New Britain and New Guinea were each too far away for planes from inland Australia to reach and return on one load of gas, the bombers took off from Cloncurry, Longreach, or Townsville, and set down either on Horn Island, a tiny spot just off the tip of Cape York, Australia, or continued on across the Torres Strait to Port Moresby located on the southern coast of New Guinea. Along the southern part of New Guinea are the towering Owen Stanley Mountains which the planes flew over to get to Lae, Salamaua, or Rabaul.

Words scarcely do justice to the Owen Stanley Mountains, which soar dramatically to more than 13,000 feet and are within a few dozen miles of Port Moresby. The lower slopes were heavily forested, so dense that daylight barely penetrated to

Chapter 3: Somewhere, Someplace, Overseas

the ground. The upper slopes were often invisible, shrouded by clouds of mist or drenching squalls. Beyond the mountains, aviators flying to Rabaul faced a long journey over the Solomon Sea, where the weather frequently turned treacherous with ultra-severe thunderstorms. Thunderheads frequently topped out at 40,000 feet or higher, well above the altitude limitations of most World War II aircraft.[3]

At the advance bases (Horn Island and Port Moresby), the planes refueled, loaded their bombs, then went on to their objective. After dropping their bombs, they returned to reload, refuel, and make necessary repairs, before embarking on another mission. On the way back from their second mission, pilots stopped at the advance base for gas, then flew back to their inland base (Cloncurry, Longreach, or Townsville). At the inland bases there were no Japanese raids, but Port Moresby was, of course, a favorite and handy target. Often returning bombers would be informed that a raid was in progress and they would have to proceed to Horn Island. "It's not the Japs so much as the distances and fatigue that worry us," one pilot said.[4]

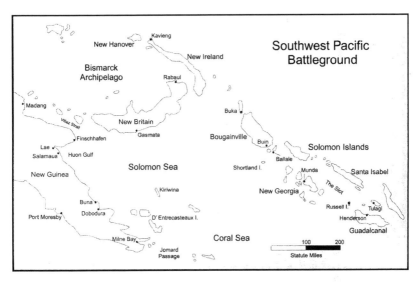

Courtesy of Bruce Gamble

19th Bomb Group: Predominant Area of Operations-1942

Although Port Moresby had a good air raid warning system, the field was totally inadequate for use by our B-17s as a full time striking base. It was impossible to conceal our big bombers at the small field. At times it resembled a parking lot. If the planes had sufficient fuel when returning to Port Moresby after completion of the mission, they would grind right on through to their bases in northeastern Australia.[5]

Horn Island (Ngurapai)

As bad as Port Moresby was, however, the airstrip at Horn Island was worse. The disadvantages at Horn Island included the ocean, the hills, and the heavy jungle forest. The island sported two runways which crossed each other in the center. The first terminated at the ocean's edge, and the other ended at the foot of

Torres Strait—Horn Island (Ngurapai)

Chapter 3: Somewhere, Someplace, Overseas

Horn Island landing field (Photo—Fran West)

the heavily forested hills. If the wind needed to give the planes lift wasn't blowing in either of the necessary directions, you had to give it everything you had and pray. A couple of times, the prayers must not have been fervent enough, for the planes kept right on into the ocean.[6]

B-17s taking off from Horn Island—1942 (Photo—Longmore)

Rabaul continued to be the primary target of the 19th BG throughout the rest of May and during the first week of June. At the same time though, Fortresses continued to hit installations on Lae and Salamaua along northern New Guinea. On June 1st one bomber hit Lae, New Guinea, but in addition to dropping bombs, the aircrews showered the areas with empty beer bottles. According to Lt. Sergeant, one of the pilots,

"Beer bottles were thrown out on the second pass which drew antiaircraft fire. Discarded purely for fun, the falling bottles made an eerie whistling sound as they twirled downward. The antiaircraft gunners, perhaps fearing that the noise was from some new type of bomb, concentrated on the whistling bottles and left the B-17s alone."[7]

Marooned

In early June, Vernon was on a night bombing raid over Rabaul. The crew encountered severe weather, which necessitated instrument flying. Tossed about, the bomber developed engine trouble before reaching the target; however, the Fortress continued toward their objective and was soon intercepted by Japanese night fighters.

The first bombing run occurred at 4000 feet, but upon inspecting the racks, the crew discovered only part of the bombs had been released. They decided to make a second run, and all the ack-ack opened up. This time, they successfully bombed the objective, but the night fighters fired from below, using the light of the bomber's engine exhaust as a target. In the ensuing action, gunners fired into the incoming enemy planes sending one flaming into the sea which caused the others to scatter. The Fortress made a steep dive, skimming over the ocean so low Japanese fighters could no longer detect the plane's location.

However, their problems were not yet over. Low on fuel, Vernon's plane had no choice but to land on the beach of a small island. The navigator determined their position by shooting the sun, and radioed the information to headquarters. Planes sent to their position dropped water, and a boat later brought fuel. After a week on this island, they took off and returned to their base.[8]

Note: Vernon, the tail gunner, was given official credit for shooting down an enemy plane, however, it's not clear it happened on this particular mission.

4
CHAPTER

Mareeba

After weeks of what seemed to be disorganization and confusion, the 19th Bomb Group started to come together as a cohesive unit. New, improved B-17Es arrived, as well as new ground crews, and the flight crews grew more experienced. However, the 19th had already fought long and hard by the time they arrived at Mareeba, and the crews felt the strain of having to fly 12-16 hour missions. Low morale became an issue.

"Mareeba was considered a god send compared to the dry, arid, and lonely bases at Longreach and Cloncurry."[1] It was also over 400 miles closer to strategic Japanese targets. Located on the Atherton Plateau, Mareeba provided an excellent environment for two runways, 6000 to 7000 feet in length. In addition, trees with overhanging branches provided much needed shade, as well as, an environment for camouflage. Nearby, the Barron River provided cool, clear water, piped to the squadron camps. Each squadron - the 28th, 30th, and 93rd - was assigned its own area of the camp, and the crewmen bathed and shaved in the river.

Crews from Mareeba flew

Preparing to land at Mareeba (Author's collection)

Port Moresby, New Guinea (Author's collection)

to Port Moresby or Horn Island, took on bombs and fuel, and continued on to targets either in New Guinea or New Britain. The bomber crews made two or three raids from these advance bases, then returned to Mareeba.[2]

"Combat crews virtually lived on the alert. In fact their very existence revolved around their aerial attacks against the enemy. As I saw it, life for them, even at the rear operational base, boiled down to preparation for, and recovery from, missions.

For 24 hours after returning from a mission, fighting airmen had no responsibilities; they could do as they chose with their time. Here again it amounted to recuperation— recuperation in preparation for the next attack. Combat crews received assignments on the average of once every 10 days or two weeks; sometimes even more frequently. Most trips lasted from two to five days, some possibly a week; the length of time depended on targets and weather conditions."[3]

The lack of supplies and spare parts for the aircraft still existed, making an extremely difficult job, next to impossible. However, the squadrons carried on the best they could, scavenging parts and cannibalizing airframes to keep other planes in the air. As General Kenney, head of the 5th Air Force, later pointed out, the aircraft of the 19th would have been withdrawn from combat in any other theater of war.

Chapter 4: Mareeba

Target Rabaul

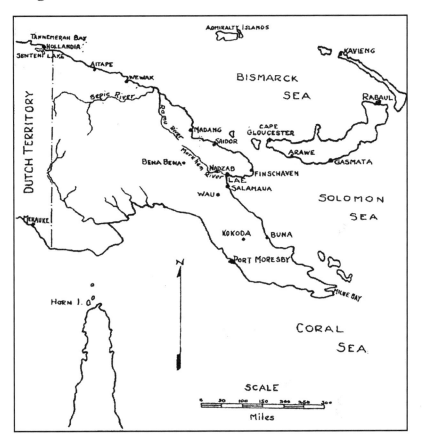

The extension of Imperial Japan's grasp on the SW Pacific hinged on the control of a physically, impenetrable stronghold located at Rabaul on the island of New Britain. Volcanoes surrounded its deep water harbor and aided the Japanese defense of this area. Because the B-17 attacks usually occurred at night, the crews often illuminated the target with incendiary bombs or dropped flares every few minutes to guide the rest of the bombers on their runs. The planes usually bombed from an altitude of between 4000 to 10,000 feet and often made individual strafing runs over the searchlight and antiaircraft positions.[4]

General Kenney aimed to diminish the Japanese strength at

Rabaul and prevent their drive toward the Solomons. Neutralizing the Japanese airfield at Vunakanau, 14 miles to the southwest, as well as, decreasing the number of Japanese forces on the Papuan Peninsula of New Guinea figured in Kenney's plan.

The initial attack on Rabaul occurred in February of 1942 when six bombers safely reached the target. While returning to base after the mission, one plane was forced to land in the swamp in New Guinea but with no casualties. It was later deemed the 'Swamp Ghost.'

Air crews were greatly challenged by missions to Rabaul.

> "If you are flying at night, swallowed by blackness; if you are tossed then dropped, it feels like the depths of hell. A feeling of powerful dread fills you; it must be dispelled by common sense. One must first, with resolution, develop confidence in instruments. In excessively turbulent weather conditions, it is possible for a plane to be tossed 3000 feet up and immediately dropped 6000 feet. Sometimes it feels as if the plane is being torn apart; one can imagine the wings ripped off, the fuselage shattered.
>
> However, often on the night raids to Rabaul, the storms had their uses. The pilots would pick out clear spots by steering between lightning flashes, which looked from the air, like long streams of fire. Thus they could pick their way between storms.
>
> But the men never got over their feeling of dread. Thunderstorms created a feeling not unlike claustrophobia. And it was nerve racking business, flying straight into blackness, with no hint of what lay ahead. Besides this menace, there was the need for making such a large proportion of their flights over water. It was true throughout this year of flying that probably twice as many planes were lost by weather as through enemy action. It was easy to understand that the greatest self-confidence was needed to overcome the uncertainty."[5]

Chapter 4: Mareeba

At this stage, the town of Mareeba tried to make the Americans feel welcome and to help them recuperate from their hair raising missions. The locals planned various social activities such as concerts, dances, and church events where Americans could mix with the community. Generally, the Americans and Aussies got along fine in and around Mareeba. However, some Aussies were known to fill bottles with tea and sell them as whiskey, but the Yanks quickly caught on to this prank.

Beer of course provided a common bond. B-17 navigator Fred Cooke recalls, "Each noon day a keg of Australian beer would be delivered to our squadron to relieve our thirst and allow relaxation; and a bread truck would deliver fresh bread each day. Our entertainment was occasional visits to Tolga and Atherton country dances."[6]

<u>NOTE</u>: *Most likely this is where Vernon met a young Australian girl named Fay Cooper. They became good friends.*

Scenes at Mareeba

*Sgt. Vernon Elder (L)
& Sgt. Rolands Boone*
(Author's collection)

Enlisted tents
(Author's collection)

The old Aussie corporal
(Author's collection)

Slit trenches
(Author's collection)

Loading the "Jersey Skeeter" for a mission.
(Author's collection)

On the way to a target
(Author's collection)

Chapter 4: Mareeba

Letters home

Vernon wrote home at least once a month. Every letter was opened by censors, a standard procedure in the war zone. He, therefore, would write in generalities asking about friends and family in La Junta, always mindful to not relate information as to location or specific missions he flew. As the weeks passed, his thoughts turn from encouragement and optimism to a sense of fatalism and fear.[7]

> May 22, 1942
> "There is a lot of the boys over here I knew in the states. You remember Houston Rice, the fellow I ran around with from Ordway (Colorado). He is in my same squadron, and we run around together."

> "You know I met a very nice girl over this way (Fay Cooper) and may have her write you a letter. Her letters are very interesting and the typical style of this country's writing."

> June 22, 1942
> "I bet it's really nice at home now, just the spring of the year. It's supposed to be the winter months over here—the seasons are just the opposite from the States."

> June 26, 1942
> "There isn't much else to say except that I'm well, and we're all doing our best over here."

> July, 1942
> "I sure would like to hear some of the new songs that are out over there now. I heard 'Deep in the Heart of Texas' for the first time. Another fellow (Henry Buller) and I bought a phonograph. It cost us 11 pounds which is about $36.00. Radios are almost priceless over here. We go to dances

where they have a three piece orchestra and is more like a barn dance. They do a lot of these old Australian dances that seem quite odd to us. The girls are getting use to our style of dancing. Hardly believe they knew what rhythm or swing was before the Yanks took over."

<u>NOTE</u>: *Some of his closest friends were Australian.*

It was during this time General Kenney flew to Mareeba to talk to Colonel Carmichael, the 19th Commander, and the men of the bomb group. The 19th BG had been kicked out of the Philippines and Java and kicked around ever since. They had had innumerable group commanders who had come and gone without leaving anything behind. The crews thought only of going home. Their morale was at a low ebb, and they didn't care who knew it.

The supply situation was appalling. Out of thirty-two B-17s at Mareeba, 18 were out of commission for lack of engines and tail wheels. About half were old model B-17s without the underneath ball turret to protect the airplane from attack from below. About the planes, General Kenney said, "They were all we had, so I had to use them if we wanted to keep the war going."[8]

Aren't you forgetting something?
(Author's collection)

Crash landing of 'Daylight Limited'
(Author's collection)

Chapter 4: Mareeba

Airman bathing camp mascot.
(Author's collection)

Above, airman rendering more dog services; right: airman displaying a local reptile.
(Author's collection)

39

Gib Guest, assistant radio man, (far right, without a hat).
(Author's collection)

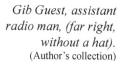

The 'Phantom' burning
(Author's collection)

Returned from bombing mission, two dead; bombardier dead in nose of plane.
(Author's collection)

5
CHAPTER

Wounded Eagle

During the month of July, there were a series of accidents on Horn Island that destroyed three B-17 bombers and severely damaged two others due to bad weather, mechanical problems, and pilot error. These accidents caused a loss of 19 airmen, 16 in one crash alone, having a traumatic impact on the 19th Bomb Group.

However, not all aircraft accidents on Horn Island were reported. Since the accidents occurred in non-combative situations, reports were sometimes not filled out or submitted.[1] For example, the following account of the crash of #655 is based primarily on Vernon's letters and interviews with Ralph Dietz, another survivor of the crash. The few official documents found also confirmed the information provided by crewmen Elder and Dietz.[2]

NOTE: Because the tail numbers used on B-17s in the SW Pacific all began with '2,' the crew often used only the last three numbers to identify a plane. Many of the bombers also had names like 'Jersey Skeeter,' 'Suzy Q,' and 'Tojo's Physic.'

"...guess we tried to be a submarine or something as we landed in the ocean"[3]

On July 14, 1942 at the early morning hour of 03:30, six Flying Fortresses lined up for takeoff on the short runway at Horn Island for a bombing mission to Lae, New Guinea. At the time, a tropical storm pounded the island. The first three bombers left without incident. However, the fourth bomber, #655 with Lt. Paul Lindsey at the controls, crashed a mile out into the Torres Strait, killing three crewmen. During takeoff, Vernon sat in the radio room. After the plane hit the water, he managed to escape through the hole the right wing created when it broke off from the fuselage.

Minutes later, the fifth bomber, #636, piloted by Lt. Curtis Holdridge, crashed off the end of the runway into the mangroves; all survived. A sixth bomber took off without incident. Because the Aussies believed Holdridge's plane was the only one that had crashed, the survivors of #655 spent an hour and a half in the water before being rescued by an Australian crash boat led by Lance Potter.[4]

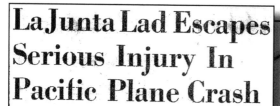

La Junta Lad Escapes Serious Injury In Pacific Plane Crash

News of an airplane crash in the Pacific theatre of operations in which Vernon Elder of La Junta was injured, Houston Rice of Ordway was killed, and Paul Lindsey of Canon City, brother of Charles Lindsey of La Junta, escaped injury was received here today by Elder's mother, Mrs. Lerenna Elder.

La Junta Dailey Tribune

Sgt. Houston Rice

Vernon wrote to his family on July 22, 1942, eight days after the crash, and reported:

> "I've been feeling a bit low this past week because my best pal was killed in a plane crash. You remember Houston Rice from Ordway, the fellow that came from Albuquerque with me when I came home that last time. I also was in the crash at the time but guess I was pretty lucky as I was only slightly cut on the face and hands but was shaken and bruised up a

Chapter 5: Wounded Eagle

bit. Guess we tried to use the plane for a submarine or something as we landed in the ocean . . . One of your last letters you asked me if I knew a Lt. Lindsey. Yes, I do know him very well; in fact, he was with Rice at the time but is okay. He certainly is one swell guy, and everyone sure does think a lot of him. We get to talking quite often about the old home state."[5]

The Crew of B-17 #655. Crashed off Horn Island – July 14, 1942

After much research, the following men were identified as being part of the crew on flight #655 the night of its crash:

Pilot: Lt. Paul M. Lindsey, Canon City, Colorado

Awarded the Distinguished Flying Cross with Oak Leaf Cluster, and the Soldiers Medal for Heroism in battle. When Lt. Lindsey flew home from his first bombing mission out of Java, 18 Japanese Zero fighters attacked his B-17. His bomber was so severely shot up, he ordered most of his crew to bail out of the disabled plane. He and his bombardier, Sgt. James Houchins, brought the plane out of an 8000 foot dive and flew into a cloud bank allowing them to escape the pursuing enemy fighters. They finally reached their base safely. After the crash off Horn Island and during their wait for rescue, Lindsey constantly called out to the surviving crewmen and went to the aid of those in need.

Co Pilot: 2nd Lt. Robert M. Kernan, West Nyack, New York

Graduated from Harvard in 1938 . . . Awarded the Soldiers Medal for Heroism in battle. After the crash, Kernan assisted an enlisted man who couldn't swim. With the help of another officer (Lindsey), they held him above water until rescued an hour and half later.[6]

Navigator: 2nd Lt. Edward R. Budz, Housatonic, Massachusetts

KIA - Horn Island, July 14, 1942. A memorial is located at the community center in Housatonic. The VFW Post 8183 is in part named after him and his brother Chester, who was a pilot in the same region. Final burial took place at St. Bridget's Cemetery in Housatonic, Massachusetts.

Bombardier: S/Sgt. James E. Houchins, Coeburn, Virginia

Was especially close to Lindsey. They had flown the 'Africa Route' together, and he flew with Lindsey on the mission out of Java where most of the crew bailed out. Houchins moved from his bombardier position to the co-pilot's seat, helped Lindsey bring the

Chapter 5: Wounded Eagle

bomber out of its spin, and made it back to base. For this, Houchins received the Distinguished Flying Cross.[7]

KIA – Horn Island, July 14, 1942
No family member met the train to receive his body when it was returned to the U.S. Final burial took place at Temple Hill Memorial Park in Castlewood, Virginia, May 10, 1949.

Ball Turret Gunner: Sgt. Edward (Ralph) Dietz, Clarion, Pennsylvania

Was ironically, not scheduled to fly on this mission. In fact, Sgt. Ralph Dietz of the 93rd Squadron had been involved 10 days earlier, July 4th, in another accident at Horn Island. His bomber # 633, later named 'Sally,' returned from a mission over Lae, New Guinea, but while landing at Horn Island, hit fuel drums on the edge of the runway, and landed with such force the left landing gear plowed up through the No. 2 engine. As a result of the crash of #633, Dietz, the bottom turret gunner, now had to return to his base by going out on another mission with #655. It is this mission that became a life or death scenario for Dietz. He said they were in shark and croc infested water for over an hour before being picked up by the Australian crash boat. Dietz described the crash as follows:

"I still reckon it was the downdraft over those mangroves. Apparently that downdraft started just after the other three took off. We hit out the farthest; the second (to go in), well he just hit off shore. A fellow tried to come out of the bomb bay, but he was whooshed back into the radio room. Then the radio operator stood up because there was an escape hatch just above us, and he was knocked down. I just said to myself, there is no use me standing up; I'll just get knocked down again. So, just about that time, the lights go out, and the water went over my head. I said to myself, if you're gonna get out of this thing, you're gonna have to try right now. So I went to stand up, and I didn't stand on anything. I reached up, and I couldn't touch anything; so I started swimming. I popped out of the water. I wasn't in the aircraft any more. I think what happened was that the fuselage was broken open where I was sitting; and then the water washed me through. I started to swim, just enough to stay on top. I couldn't see the shoreline; it was too dark. I just started paddling, but the current kept taking me down. Lindsey kept yelling "93rd", "93rd" to check up on me. Then the crash boat came out . . . for the second plane that went in. They didn't know we were out there. The other fellows were hollering out, so the Australian crash boat picked them up; then they picked me up. They all didn't get out . . . There were two fellows that were trapped in the airplane, and they went down with it; and the other fellow, they knew he was dead because they brought his body in."[8]

Ralph Dietz (far right) and other 93rd crewmates. Mareeba, QLD

Chapter 5: Wounded Eagle

Flight Engineer/Gunner: Sgt. Houston A. Rice, Ordway, Colorado

KIA – Horn Island, July 14, 1942. His final burial, with full Military Honors, took place at Golden Gate National Cemetery in San Bruno, California, May 1949.

Sgt. Rice taken in Australia shortly before the fatal crash. (courtesy of Renee Wingerd)

One of three crewmen who died in the crash of # 655. Thus the 'Colorado Connection' lost one of its own. Houston was not scheduled to fly this mission, but Lt. Lindsey, the pilot, needed a man, so he volunteered. This came as no surprise to his fellow crewmen who knew of his profound loyalty. As Vernon pointed out later…"that's just the kind of man he was." The surviving members of the 'Colorado Connection,' Paul Lindsey and Vernon, kept Rice afloat until an Australian crash boat rescued them.

Aboard the rescue crash boat that night, Australian Lance Potter pulled men out of the water. An entry in his diary stated:

"A plane is down, and we have to rush out to rescue. Approx. 3:30 am Tuesday, away we go in crash boat, Sol driving, me on searchlight. We travel three miles or so and find wreckage. Stopping engines we call out and listen for answering cries. Yes, there they are; so we shine the beam inshore. Airmen wade toward us in water about four feet deep dragging something. Coming closer we help them on. One man is dead (Rice); we leave him on the cockpit floor. The other men are wet and cold after being in the water over an hour. They say there is another plane down also. One man has a badly gashed leg; we get out med kit and soon have tourniquet and are making back for base. We meet Ross in bomb scow, and I go with him and the Captain (Lindsey) of the plane; and we search for the other plane. We soon find it in about 10 feet of water and begin to punch the Perspex in to see if there is anybody in the forward turret. After doing so we begin to search the sea. We stop the engines of the scow and decide to wait until daylight. Dawn comes and so we make back towards the wreck. Make thorough examination and find mostly in tack but back broken and one engine missing."[9]

Australian crash boat that picked up crew members (Photo by Lance Potter)

Tail Gunner: S/Sgt. Vernon O. Elder, La Junta, Colorado

Injured in the crash of #655 on Horn Island, July 14, 1942. A year later he wrote a letter to a friend giving this account of the crash:

"The end of the runway was right at the end of the beach, and as soon as you got off the ground you were over the ocean. We got off the ground ok and were about 200 ft. high, wheels up, and motors doing ok. We were indicating about 140 and about a mile off shore. For no apparent reason we started to go down; the old plane just wouldn't climb.

Chapter 5: Wounded Eagle

We really hit the water, and it was an experience I'll never forget. I was in the radio compartment and went through the right side of the fuselage. Bruised and cut me up pretty bad but nothing very serious. Rice was by the ball turret and was apparently killed instantly, as he had a bad looking place on his right temple. That was the only place."[10]

Vernon was awarded the Silver Star with Oak Leaf Cluster, and Air Medal for action over Java, Coral Sea, New Guinea, and the Solomons. He earned credit for shooting down a Japanese Zero fighter plane. Returning from another mission, his plane ran low on gas, and the pilot performed an emergency landing on a small island.

Vernon was buried with full Military Honors at Fort Logan National Cemetery in Denver, Colorado, March 27, 1973.

Cloncurry Air Base, April, 1942

Mareeba Air Base, November, 1942

Waist gunner: Sgt. Henry Buller, Billings, Montana

On takeoff Sgt. Buller sat in the radio room with Elder, Deitz and Rice, and all washed out into the ocean. According to Dietz there were sharks in the area; and he was bleeding, as were most of the others. Buller swam back to the wreckage, which was mostly underwater, and retrieved their shark repellant. Buller was six-foot-five, and the waist gunner position best fit his height.[11] He received the Silver Star, and Oak Leaf Cluster and earned credit for shooting down a Japanese Zero on June 1, 1942 over Rabaul. Buller flew on the mission with Vernon where they ended up marooned on a small island. Buller and Elder were good friends and bought a phonograph together for $36.00. They were also crewmates on the very successful raid on Rabaul, August 7, 1942. Their pilot on that mission was Lt. Curtis Holdridge.

Sgt. Buller; pictured in Menace from Moresby

l-r. Elder, ? Buller, ?, at Mareeba

Chapter 5: Wounded Eagle

NOTE: All three casualties of the crash of #655—Rice, Budz, and Houchins—were placed in adjoining burial sites on Thursday Island, approximately three miles from Horn Island. An Australian chaplain, Archie Harris, conducted the services for the three American flyers on July 15-16, 1942. Vernon attended the burials of his fellow crewmates, though most of those present were Australians.[12] The Australians later exhumed the bodies and relocated them to Townsville.

Throughout the war, the Australian government treated the fallen with dignity, and assured the continuous care of the heroic Americans who died in the service of their country and in the defense of Australia. After the war, the Australian's either placed their remains in permanent American cemeteries overseas or returned them to the U.S. for final burial. The three men who died on #655 came home to their families in 1949.

The survivors of the crash of #655 were given a 10-day pass. Vernon told his family it felt more like a vacation to see the city lights and go dancing. No doubt he was mindful not to share the details of his crash with his family, but he did mention Lindsey accompanied them on this well-deserved leave.

NOTE: Vernon soon flew on the single biggest mission the 19th conducted over the fiercely defended Rabaul. The Eagle Dancer from La Junta, Colorado, danced on the 'Thunder Drum' again.

Vernon's next letter said his tent had accidently burned down, and he had lost some photos and souvenirs he planned to send home. He also shared these revealing comments:

> "Everything is going along very well for me, and I'm feeling fine now since the accident. The only thing is I'm still a bit nervous, but it shouldn't last long. If it keeps up I may have to quit flying for a little while. Guess I was pretty lucky to get out of the crash as easy as I did."[13]

Other Costly Crashes on Horn Island

The biggest single tragedy on Horn Island was the crash of B-17 #421 piloted by Major Clarence MacPherson on July 16, 1942. They were transporting a salvage crew and replacement parts — landing gear, propellers, brake assembly and tools — for the repair of the 'Sally,' which had collapsed a landing gear two weeks earlier. According to eyewitness accounts, there was windy weather and darkening skies. Upon approach, #421 took the wrong side of the flares and tried to pull up and turn. This maneuver caused the loose, heavy equipment to shift. The plane dove and exploded killing all 16 aboard.

One of the most popular crewmen aboard that fateful evening was M/Sgt. 'Soup' Silva, who was respected and liked by all who knew him. He was not scheduled to go on the trip, but the crew needed someone who knew how to light the flares at Mareeba for the return flight. This marked the largest wartime aviation disaster that Horn Island experienced.[14]

Eleven days later another accident at Horn Island, caused purely by pilot error, took out two more B-17s. After a predawn landing, the Fortress, piloted by 2nd Lt. Edward Bechtold was taxiing, and a wing clipped the nose of B-17 'Tojo's Physic,' piloted by Lt. Carey O'Bryan. Later, 19th BG Commander Rouse commented:

> "Bechtold ground-looped on landing and tore the nose completely off one of our ships and smashed his pretty badly – purely pilot error due to inexperience, I believe. Two more ships gone that we badly needed." [15]

This traumatic month, with terrible losses in both human life and planes, led to the continued drop in morale for the war-weary 19th BG airmen.

Chapter 5: Wounded Eagle

Great Raid on Rabaul - August 7, 1942

Vernon was still recovering from his injuries when the 30th Squadron took part in the largest assault on Rabaul. Japan now controlled the former British base on the island of New Britain, and from it launched their offensive operations against Guadacanal and Tulagi. Japan took full advantage of the surrounding volcanic terrain to protect their large fleet.

Within close distance, several Japanese air bases provided a formidable defense for the harbor, and antiaircraft defenses were prolific. Any air attack on Rabual had to be from a high altitude or a corkscrew approach at lower altitudes.

Even with these challenges, General Kenney ordered the bombing of Rabaul in conjunction with the Marine landings at Guadacanal and Tulagi. The 19th Bomb Group departed from its base at Mareeba and staged through Port Moresby on New Guinea. Of the 16 bombers that left Mareeba, three never reached the final formation at Port Moresby. Because of mechanical problems, one veered off the runway on takeoff, and the other two had engine trouble, forcing a return to base.

Capt. Harl Pease piloted one of the returning planes. The only other B-17 available at Mareeba had been deemed 'not combat-worthy' because of electrical problems and weak engines, but Pease declared it combat-worthy and took off to rejoin the 93rd Squadron at Port Moresby.

In the early hours of August 7th, the large formation of B-17s left Port Moresby headed toward Rabaul and the large air base at Vunakanau. Flying at 22,000 feet, 20 enemy fighters intercepted them. The pilots of the Zeroes were the best Japan had; most were veterans of years of combat in China and throughout the Far East. However, despite damage from gunfire, the B-17s continued on their bombing run.

Although it was always the tail gunner the Japanese went after first, Vernon, Lt. Holdridge's tail gunner, survived the fierce battle and was credited with shooting down an enemy aircraft.

For this accomplishment, General Kenney later presented him the Silver Star, America's third highest award for valor.

However, Capt. Pease and his crew were not so lucky. Because of his late arrival at Port Moresby, Pease was assigned 'Tail End Charley,' the most vulnerable position in the formation. During the flight to the target, his plane dropped behind, and the Japanese fighters concentrated on the straggler. Witnesses watched Pease's bomber go down with two engines on fire.

Some people believed Pease and another crewman survived the crash, but were captured by the Japanese and later executed. No one ever questioned, however, Pease's determination to be part of the biggest raid, up to that time, against the Japanese on New Britain. Because of his heroism, Pease was later awarded the Congressional Medal of Honor.

George Weller reported in an article for the *Chicago Daily News*:

". . . boy I'd like to sock anybody who says anything against our bombing after this," says one officer. "I never saw a better bombing anywhere. We laid three absolutely perfect strings down that concrete runway - one to the right, one to the left, and one in the middle." The nearest plane is snorting to a stop. It is commanded by Lt. Curtis Holdridge of Aldero, Oklahoma and Lt. Hiram Messmore of Lincoln, Nebraska; with John Crockett of Stephens, Arkansas; S/Sgt Stanley Jackola of Minneapolis, Minn.; Victor Lorber of Syracuse; Vernon Elder of La Junta, Colorado; Henry Buller, of Billings, Montana; and J. W. Hanns of South Bend, Indiana. Here come more and more men clapping each other upon the back."[16]

General Kenney, duly proud of his airmen, later wrote:

Chapter 5: Wounded Eagle

". . . the kids closed up their formation and fought their way to Vunakanau where they dropped their bombs in a group pattern that was a bull's eye. The 150 Japanese planes were still beside the runway as ninety-six 500 lb. bombs fell on the airfield. The pictures looked as though we got at least 75 of them, besides setting fire to a lot of gasoline and blowing up a big bomb dump on the edge of the field."[17]

The most important effect of this mission was the prevention of Japanese air action against the Marine landing at Guadacanal, but it also served as a tremendous morale boost for the battered 19th BG.

Flare Test Tragedy

On the night of August 16th, a specially equipped B-17 with a volunteer crew of 12, took off from Mareeba, 23 miles east of Cairns, Australia. The purpose of the mission was to test magnesium flares that could be used to light up targets for better visual during bombing runs. Lt. Paul Lindsey piloted the plane. Also on board that night was Major Dean 'Pinky' Hoevet, commander of the 30th Bomb Squadron, and an engineering and technical crew to evaluate the new device. One of the magnesium flares got caught in the bomb bay and prematurely ignited. Lindsey tried to make an emergency landing at Cairns airport, but didn't have good control of the plane. To avoid a crash landing in the city, he put the plane down in the water off the coast near Yorkey's Knob. All perished in the crash; and six crewmen were never recovered, including Lindsey.

A large memorial service was held at 2:00 p.m. on the lawn of the Cairns city hall with virtually the entire community attending. An honor guard of three—an Australian soldier, an Australian sailor, and an American soldier—stood at attention near the six caskets. Silently the citizens of Cairns and Australian and American military personnel, passed through the room.

There were groups from the Australian Navy, Air Force, Army, and Nurses Corps, as well as, American soldiers and hundreds of Australian civilians. Australian flags flew at half-mast throughout the town, and the American flag flew on the city hall flagpole. Mr. Collins, a citizen of Cairns, sang a solo, 'The Trumpeter.' A firing squad of 12 American soldiers faced the ocean toward America and fired their salutes. As the sound of the volleys died away, Taps were sounded, and the pallbearers carried the coffins into the city hall. Saturday the coffins were put on a train for Townsville where the burial took place.[18]

Lt. Bob Wasson later remarked:

"Lindsey never drank much; he didn't smoke and seldom worried. But I remember after three of his crewmen were drown in that water crackup off Australia (Horn Island), he was about to admit he was jinxed. He sipped a couple of beers slowly that night and told us he was damn sure it was 'total war,' but he kept flying anyway." [19]

Today Lindsey is listed on 'Tablets of the Missing' at Manila American Cemetery, Manilla, Philippines.

<u>NOTE:</u> *Now Vernon was the sole surviving member of the 'Colorado Connection.' No wonder he was 'nervous to fly.'*

Paul's sister, Doris, recalled, "When our parents received the missing-in-action telegram, they were inconsolable in their grief. Our close-knit family now had one missing member forever."[20]

In letters written by Vernon during September and October, he described his

Lt. Paul Lindsey, 1941

Chapter 5: Wounded Eagle

Paul Lindsey as a student at Colorado A&M, 1937 (Lindsey photos courtesy of Bonnie Quiggle, niece of Lindsey)

feelings about the loss of his friend and fellow crewman, Paul Lindsey:

September 1, 1942

"I don't know if you've heard or not, but you can tell George that his school teacher's brother isn't with us anymore. It happened soon after we were on that leave of ours. He was with us you know; I believe I wrote you about it not so long ago."[21]

<u>NOTE:</u> *Charles Lindsey, brother of Paul, taught at La Junta High School at the time. Vernon's nephew, George Elder, was a student in Charles' class.*

October 4, 1942

"I know how Mrs. Lindsey must feel about her son, Paul. He was certainly a swell fellow, and we all miss him very much. Don't know what the paper said about it, but I do know how it happened, where etc.; of course I can't write about such things, though."[22]

Echoes From an Eagle

October 19, 1942

"I would like to write to Mrs. Lindsey, but any information I could give her about Paul would be censored. However, she should receive all the information and details concerning Paul from the gov't, and possibly she has got that information by this time."[23]

"Some Australian friends of mine have invited me to tea Thursday evening and are making me a birthday cake. I'm not doing so bad am I?"

"We had quite a ceremony the other afternoon. A General presented a lot of us with our medals and tacked them on our chest. He even saluted us first and then shook our hands. That's something quite unusual."[24]

Sgt. Vernon Elder's torn and water damaged watch stopped at 03:34. His bomber took off from Horn Island at 03:30 into a severe tropical storm. It crashed a mile out into the ocean. He was in the water for an hour holding on to his best friend before an Australian crash boat picked up the survivors. (Author's collection)

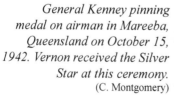

General Kenney pinning medal on airman in Mareeba, Queensland on October 15, 1942. Vernon received the Silver Star at this ceremony.
(C. Montgomery)

Chapter 5: Wounded Eagle

In a V-mail sent by Vernon to his mother and his sister, Mildred, dated October 23rd, they received the first clue that what they had hoped and prayed for might soon happen. He writes:

> "Mildred, I don't believe I'd send any more records for a while because for certain reasons might not get them. If for any reason you don't hear from me for a while, don't be alarmed . . . who knows, there might be a pleasant surprise for you one of these days."[25]

Nov 21, 1942 in a letter written home, Vernon said:

> "I had some more good news the other day. Quite a number of us boys are getting the Distinguished Flying Cross award. We haven't received them yet, but the orders are out; so we will probably get them soon."[26]

<u>NOTE:</u> *Vernon never received his Distinguished Flying Cross. Unfortunately, many 19th BG records were lost, misplaced, or accidently destroyed during the demanding days of 1942. The priority was to keep the Fortresses air worthy and prevent the Japanese from establishing a major foothold in eastern New Guinea and the Bismarck Archipelago.*

"From One Anxious Mother to Another"

Throughout the 19th BG's deployment to Java and Australia, family members of those flying long, dangerous bombing missions only received information through newspapers and radio reports. When they received letters from their far away airmen, information was shared through personal letters between anxious mothers. My grandmother, Lerenna Elder, received the following letters from Mrs. Fred Messmore and Mrs. Sue Crockett.[27]

Written by Mrs. Fred Messmore, wife of Nebraska Supreme

Echoes From an Eagle

Court Justice, the Honorable Fred W. Messmore:

To the family of Vernon Elder, La Junta, Colorado

August 15, 1942

I am enclosing an exact copy of an article appearing in the Chicago Daily News – in which Vernon Elder is mentioned as being on the heaviest raid on Rabaul also on the same bomber as our son Lieut. Hiram Messmore. My husband had several copies made, we thought you might like one. Our last news of our son was June 20th. He made his escape from the Philippines in April and has been over there since May 8, 1941.

Trusting God is always with our boys on their missions

I am sincerely,
Mrs. Fred Messmore

To Lerena Elder

Sept. 19, 1942

Dear Mrs. Elder,

Mr. Messmore and I are wondering if you have heard from Vernon since the first raid on Rabaul? Our last letter from Hiram was before—We are so anxious to hear—since there is so much fighting still going on in that area. From one anxious mother to another.

Sincerely,
Mrs. Fred Messmore, Lincoln, Nebr.

Chapter 5: Wounded Eagle

Written by Mrs. Sue Crocket, mother of John Crockett from Stephens, Arkansas.

To Lerena Elder,

Oct. 12, 1942

Dear Mrs. Elder,

I was happy to hear from you again and appreciate the clipping very much. You are very lucky to hear from your son so recently. I had a letter today from Al written August 14. In it he said he had not heard from me since April – though I've been writing twice each week. They seem to be doing a fine job over there. I'd give anything if I could go too. I have heard that the 30th Bomb Sqd. is to be sent home before Xmas for a rest – another thing did you know that they will be given some honor medal for bombing Rabaul the first time. I hope that God will continue to keep them all safe.

Best wishes to you.
Sue Crockett

Coming Home

By October of 1942 the 19th Bomb Group had been engaged in combat for 10 months. The bomber crewmen were long ago battle tested, and they were seasoned veterans. But after the Java experience and resurrecting an offensive strike force in Australia, they were exhausted. Their B-17s had worn out before their time, and the flight crews suffered from combat fatigue because of serving too long in hazardous environments, with no end in sight. The U. S. command under General George Kenney recognized the predicament of the veterans of the 19th, and decided to relieve the Group from combat as soon as replacement units could take over.

During this time, the 19th began departing for the U.S. Those personnel who had the most time in the war zone returned to the U.S. first. In the third week of October, 12 Fortresses loaded with 19th personnel left Australia via Hawaii and were homeward bound. On November 29th the remainder departed Townsville aboard the *USTS Torrens* for their long journey across the Pacific. They were finally going home. The ship took a more southerly route to avoid any possible contact with the Japanese. Vernon, bed ridden with yellow jaundice, was a passenger aboard ship.

USTS Torrens (Australian War Memorial)

Some of our boys on ship coming home
(Author's collection)

Chapter 5: Wounded Eagle

Returning from Australia
(Author's collection)

Entering San Francisco Harbor after 18 nonstop days at sea
(Author's collection)

After eighteen straight days crossing the Pacific, the *Torrens* arrived in San Francisco. Vernon had to be hospitalized and treated by Army doctors. In a letter he wrote from Letterman Hospital in San Francisco, Vernon reported:

". . . what a pleasant sight it was to sail under the Golden Gate Bridge, although the weather was typical San Francisco, foggy and rainy. We all about froze to death because we've been used to the hot climate . . . it's certainly going to seem strange to sleep in a bed with a mattress, springs and clean sheets. All I've had ever since I left has been an army cot and army blankets, and many a time we've slept under the wing of our airplane with just our flying suits . . . while on my way over here on the boat, I got what they call 'yellow

63

jaundice.' It's caused by improper diet. Your eyeballs turn slightly yellow and also the skin. The doctors say I will be alright with some rest." [28]

In a telegram to his mother:
"...leaving hospital tomorrow for Pocatello, Idaho, hope to see you soon."[29]

During Vernon's furlough, his hometown of La Junta, treated him as a hero. He was a special guest speaker at the McFarland American Legion Post #9. A large gathering attended to hear him describe two of his dangerous missions over Rabaul, including his being marooned for a week on a small island in the Torres Strait.

This young man had been born and raised in this community, and they had seen him perform as the Koshare Eagle Dancer on the 'Thunder Drum.' The dance portrayed a trapped eagle that screamed loudly before its death. But this time the eagle (Vernon) had luckily escaped the trap and lived to dance again.

After nearly eight months of combat in the skies over Java, New Guinea, and New Britain, the 19th Bomb Group came home. They were the first to fly B-17s in combat against the Japanese, nine months before the planes were operational in Europe. During this period, ground crews and airmen made needed modifications to the gun positions, including a manned belly gun and more effective mounted machine guns in the nose and tail. These modifications gave the bomber more defensive fire power but required the crews to learn quickly in a combat atmosphere. As if they did not have enough challenges, their missions were 8-10 hours long, often flying through violent and unpredictable tropical storms. They also encountered battle-tested Japanese Zeroes.

Vernon had endured over 40 long missions in the freezing cold while wearing bulky suits and an oxygen mask. He had survived a crash into the ocean that injured him and took the life

Chapter 5: Wounded Ea[g]

of his best friend, Houston Rice, as well as
landing on a remote island. A month after
lost his other Colorado buddy, Lt. Paul Li[n]
fear, dread, and death, Vernon's youth and
forever. He now had scars inside and ou...
and friends expected him to be the same person who had
war. Because of the lack of true understanding of what he had
experienced and his inability to tell them, there would be stress
and conflict for all of those in Vernon's life.

<u>NOTE</u>: *Like the old B-17s, the 19th Bomb Group was finally retired and sent home in late 1942. The19th came back to the Pacific with fresh crews and flying the new B-29s; but this time, they headed toward Japan*

19th Bomb Group Officers
Front: L-R: Chiles, Young, Maddux, Swanbeck, O'Bryan, Norvell, Beekman
Middle: L-R: Hinton, Cappelletti, Hohmann, unk, Harris, Nanny, Snyder, McAullife
Back: L-R: Smith, Work, Cottage, Becktold, Railey, Jaquet, Miller
(Courtesy of Dr. Bob O'Bryan, son of Lt. Carey O'Bryan Jr.)

Above: Seen at low tide, the remaining engine of a B-17 (#636 in the map below) that crashed the same day as Vernon's plane (#655). Below: map showing the two crash sites off Horn Island. (Engine photo courtesy of Liberty and Vanessa Seekee)

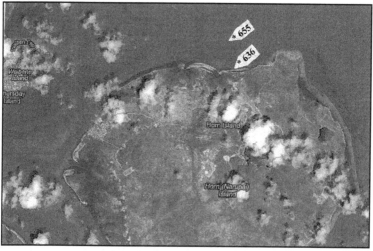

6
CHAPTER

Rattlesnake Bomber Base

Of the thousands of men in the 19th BG who went to the Philippines or Java in late 1941 and flew missions over New Guinea and Rabaul in 1942, only 161 arrived at Pyote's 'Rattlesnake Bomber Base,' the new home of the 19th Bombardment Group.[1] The unit had been awarded four Distinguished Unit Citations, one of which recounted the group's heroic fight to provide cover for the Marines when they landed at Guadacanal.

When the men of the 19th arrived in the cactus and coyote country of West Texas, they soon became the nucleus for the training of a new generation of pilots, navigators, and bombardiers who would fly improved versions of the B-17, the new 'Super Fortress' B-29. The experience gained in combat operations in Java and the SW Pacific, served as the foundation for the new trainees. The base, better known as 'Rattlesnake' Bomber Base, encompassed a 3000-acre installation named after its most pervasive local reptile. It soon became the largest bomber base in the country. In these vast, remote stretches of the Southwest, the weather forecast often included wind, dust storms, and snow for the same day.

Public Relations, Pyote Air Base

Public Relations, Pyote Air Base

Military discipline and courtesy were not a priority for men who had just returned from life and death experiences in the skies over New Guinea and New Britain. They were not keen on the pomp and circumstance involved in by-the-book, military discipline. Their battle savvy and dedication to the goal of winning the war defined the 19th Bombardment Group.[2]

Vernon, one of 18 members of the historic 19th BG, received the Air Medal for meritorious achievement. These medals were presented to those airmen who had participated in operational flights where exposure to enemy fire was probable and expected.[3] The Air Medal joined Vernon's previously awarded Silver Star with Oak Leaf Cluster.

After his arrival at Pyote, Vernon and my mother, Mary Daley, rekindled the relationship that had begun in Albuquerque. The 19th had been stationed at Kirtland Field, and my mother attended the University of New Mexico. Throughout Vernon's deployment in Java and Australia, they kept in touch through letters, though most of them arrived a month after being mailed. On April 24, 1943 they were married in Monahans, Texas, about

Chapter 6: Rattlesnake Bomber Base

Vernon (1st on left) and his fellow 19th veteran airmen receiving their Air Medals at Pyote Air Base (Author's collection)

My first home in Monahans, Texas
(Author's collection)

Vernon, my mom, T.J. Rice
(Author's collection)

15 miles from the base, and rented a small house in Monahans. I arrived in April of 1944.

<u>NOTE</u>: Years later my mother told me about the horrific dust storms that often hit the area. During the summer, she'd wet a towel and hang it in an open window to cool the hot, dry air. This was her idea of a poor man's swamp cooler.

On the base, Vernon trained bombardiers and headed up security for the Norden bombsight building. As the non-commissioned officer in charge, he and his staff had to have a high aptitude for understanding and working with mechanical devices. After each completed training mission, the bombsight was removed, placed in a bag, and deposited in a concrete hardened vault. This was one of the most technically skilled ground echelon jobs, and certainly, one of the most secret.

The veterans of the 19th were hardened, but tired, and had little time to rest. They had a job to do. Their combat experience proved invaluable, and they flew training missions with the new air crews. Success in the preparation of these new crewmen rested on their shoulders. The urgent need for combat ready crews during 1943 and into 1944 dramatically increased the number of training missions they had to fly. The records at Pyote were unequaled elsewhere throughout the war. However, maintaining the air-worthiness of each B-17 at this pace, presented a challenge. Fatal crashes became routine. Within a seven week period, three Fortresses crashed resulting in the death of 24 crewmen.[4]

As the war in Europe began to wind down, more attention and effort was directed toward the Pacific Theater. A new strategic bomber, the B-29 'Super Fortress,' started to phase out the older Flying Fortresses. In the words of aviation historian, Edward Jablonski:

"The B-17 had served, unlike any other heavy bomber,

Chapter 6: Rattlesnake Bomber Base

through all of the Second World War. It had become a legend in its time; a tribute to the men who had conceived, designed, and built it; and a monument to the men, most of them boys, who flew it. These men, and this plane accomplished one of the most frightening missions ever demanded of men and aircraft. Together they helped to end history's last "Glorious War."[5]

The new B-29s had the capacity for a 10,000 pound payload and a range of 6000 miles as compared to the 3300-4400 mile range of the older model B-17G. Single training missions, often lasting for 23 1/2 hours, resulted in a very long day for the crews, but the hours were necessary to prepare for the upcoming strikes on the Japanese home islands. Vernon flew on many of these long missions as a Norden bomb sight instructor. According to my mother, he often flew from Pyote to the Canadian border, then east toward New York, and then back to Pyote.

As islands in the Pacific fell to the Americans and distance to the Japanese mainland decreased, the 'Super Fortresses' became more effective. This was especially true when the bombings occurred at night and at the lower, but more risky, 5000 to 10,000 feet altitude, with the planes dropping incendiary bombs. In one raid alone, B-29s dropped 1667 tons of these incendiary bombs on Tokyo, destroying 15 square miles in the heart of the capital city. The next night, 300 B-29s destroyed another 25 percent of the city. The instructors and support personnel back at Pyote were filled with pride at what their crews accomplished, and the crews in the skies over Tokyo were thankful they had learned so very well their deadly skills of war.[6]

Last Mission

On August 6, 1945, Col. Paul Tibbetts sat at the controls of the B-29 'Enola Gay,' named for his mother. He led a mission that would forever change the history of warfare. Even his crewmen were unaware of the single 'atomic bomb' that was to be dropped on the city of Hiroshima, Japan. For three days after the bombing, the American leaders expected an announcement of surrender from the Japanese High Command. However, the surrender ultimatum went ignored. A second, more powerful bomb fell on the coastal city of Nagasaki on August 9th. Shortly thereafter, the Japanese surrendered unconditionally.

News of the surrender quickly spread throughout the 'Rattlesnake' Base community. Compared to other cities around the country, the celebrations in Pyote and Monahans were rather muted. Despite the surrender, training continued with more than 6000 hours of flight time logged for August, and by this time the base employed over 8000 military personnel and civilians. As they continued their duties, the veteran airmen hoped they would soon be released, and that the more recent recruits would continue with base functions.[7]

By way of recognizing the valorous service of the 19th BG whose men had been among the first to face the enemy, the War Department declared that anyone who served on Wake, Guam, the Dutch East Indies, or the Philippines prior to May 1942 was eligible for immediate discharge. The 84 members of the original 19th still at Pyote on VJ Day were thus, unquestionably, qualified to leave the service, even though, their departure would create large holes in the training staff.[8]

Unfinished Business

While at Pyote, Vernon struggled to come to grips with the death of his best friend, Houston Rice. He and Houston had been together throughout their training days at March Field in California and Kirtland Field in Albuquerque. When given a pass off base, they headed into town to enjoy the movies, cafes, and dance halls. The rumor among the local girls was that Houston and Vernon were pretty good dancers.

Houston's death, therefore, was one of the most traumatic loss-

Chapter 6: Rattlesnake Bomber Base

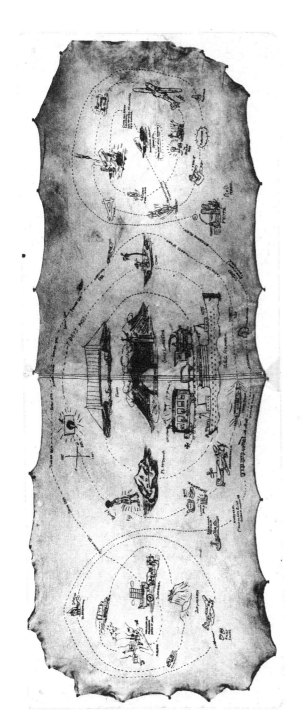

Buffalo Hide Calendar:
This visual depiction, drawn on hide, was found among Vernon's letters. The spiral method of recording events was a tradition among the Plains Indians. It is consistent with the location and history of the 19th Bomb Group in 1942. The drawing and printing is quite similar to Vernon's own hand, however, the route and some of the events cannot be attributed to him. To follow in chronological order start in the center and read counter clockwise following the dotted lines

es for Vernon during his time at war. Whether the two friends shared a pact or not, Vernon felt compelled to contact John Rice, Houston's father, to give him a firsthand account of how his son died. Vernon also had some of the last pictures taken of Houston that he wanted to pass on to the family.

However, this desire to help the Rice family find closure for their grief, turned out to be a difficult task. The family had moved from Ordway, Colorado while Houston was overseas, and Vernon didn't know where they had settled. Evidently, he finally located them because the shoe box full of letters included Mr. Rice's response to Vernon:

September 11, 1943

Dear Friend Mr. Elder,

   I can't express in words how glad I am to get your letter and pictures of my son Houston. I have been hoping and trusting that I could some time get in touch with some of you boys that were with him at the time of his death so I could get the facts about it. It is such a great consolation to know that his body was recovered and put away with a funeral for I know a lot of them didn't get (even) that much. Houston was very very dear to me and I just can't get over losing him. I guess it will always seem like he will be home some time. But one consolation Houston liked the (army) the last time I saw him he said Daddy I never intend to do anything only stay with the army and thought so much of the fellows he was with always giving the boys praise for something you had done for him. Yes I have heard him speak of you lots of time It seems as though you was his closest friend. He liked them all. I am glad you sent the snap shots as they look just like him. The Govment sent his personal belongings home and his camera had a roll of Film in it with some shots already taken so I had them Developed they were taken on a Rocky stream looks like I suppose out there somewhere. They sent a bill of laden

Chapter 6: Rattlesnake Bomber Base

of his personal belongings and his watch was on it but when the things came his watch was not in it. I would of liked to have his watch most of all as it would have been the best keep sake of anything he had. Houston gave us a big picture of his with his uniform on and the last time he was here he got it said he wanted to give it to his girl so do you know who it was or where I could get in touch with her, I sure would like to get me one made of that one I thought it looked so much like him and know weather Houston carried any insurance or not I wrote to the Ins. Department about it and they said they would investigate and as quick as they find out they would write me but I never have heard and there is one more thing Vernon. I <u>would</u> like for you to tell me did they put the body in a coffin of any kind or do they just wrap them in a tarpaulin and put them away. Well Vernon I guess I have wrote enough for this time. You will never know just how much your letter means to me and what a joy comfort it is to know the things you have told me for I would of always been wondering if they recover his body or if he had any funeral but now it is all cleared up. And I thank you more than I can tell and I feel so good that you can give Houston such good praise for his work and as a friend. I will keep and cherish your letter as long as I live. I have got two more boys in the service Lester is at Camp Roberts and John Dean is in the navy on the U.SS. Tennessee. Donald is 18 will be going soon I guess. 4 of them Houston was the oldest. I am working here in the shipyards as welder. I hope here soon we can clean up those rats so all our boys can come home. Please write me again and I wish you all the good luck a man can have and thanks for writing us.
 Your friend John W. Rice[9]

John Rice's letter to my father, written with such moving sincerity, not only reflected his pain at losing Houston, but also his profound gratitude for information that brought some closure to his grief.

NOTE: *As I read Rice's letter, I considered the possibility of finding Vernon's original letter to John. What could I learn about my own father by words written when he was only 24, describing his best friend's death?*

Moving On

As one of the original airmen of the 19th BG with nearly six years of service including combat in Java and the SW Pacific, Vernon received an honorable discharge from the Army Air Corps in September 1945. He had flown half way around the world, immediately experienced aerial combat against the Japanese, lost two of his best friends, and survived a plane crash. Vernon completed his service as a decorated veteran and returned home to begin his search for 'normalcy.'

Soon after Vernon's discharge, my family left Monahans. Finally, he could put away his uniform and find a way to transition back into a world he left so long ago.

We first went to visit my maternal grandparents in Grants, New Mexico. After a short stay with them, we went to Glendale, California where Vernon worked at a small hotel owned by one of his friends. For some reason that job didn't work out, so a year later, we were back in New Mexico, but my parents' marriage was not going well. My mother and I remained in New Mexico with her parents while Vernon returned to his family and friends in La Junta, Colorado. My parents tried to work out their differences, but by 1948, decided against reconciliation and filed for divorce.

Perhaps my father was not the same person after his year overseas. What man would come back unchanged after such traumatic war experiences? Vernon wanted only to return to his hometown, work at a non-threatening job, and enjoy peaceful excursions into the plains of southeastern Colorado. As he stated

Chapter 6: Rattlesnake Bomber Base

in one of his letters from Australia, ". . . I've had enough thrills and excitement to do me the rest of my life."

As a three year old boy, 1947 proved to be a very scary, confusing, and lonely period in my life. I seldom saw my dad, and I missed him. I never understood why he no longer lived with us. Also, because Mom had to work to support us, I was often left with people I didn't know well. This added to my feeling of loneliness and disorientation.

Then in November 1948, Mom married my stepfather, Bill Bledsoe. He was also a WWII veteran and worked for the Civil Aeronautics Administration (CAA). After their wedding, we moved to Zuni, New Mexico where he helped operate a small communication and weather station.

Vernon also remarried in December 1948. My stepmother wasn't crazy about having kids around, so visiting my dad became even more difficult. However, once or twice a year, Grandmother Elder would board the train from La Junta to Albuquerque, pick me up, and take me back to her home. Those visits were filled with picking strawberries in her garden, picnics with my Aunt Mildred and cousins, and time with my dad. Then Grandmother and I would get on the train and head back to Albuquerque. Those were fun times but were never long enough to really get to know my dad.

After leaving Zuni in 1950, my mom, stepdad, and I moved to the Panama Canal Zone for two years. My stepdad continued to work for the CAA, and Mom also had a job with the U.S. government.

I turned six while we were there and started first grade. Unfortunately, I also contracted polio that same year and had to be hospitalized. No longer able to walk, I endured months of extensive rehab and exercises. I was one of the lucky ones, though, because eventually, I began to improve and regain the use of my legs.

In 1951, we moved back to New Mexico. I was admitted to Carrie Tingley Hospital in Hot Springs (Truth or Consequences), to continue my rehab and recovery. Upon my release from the hospital, we moved to Albuquerque, and that fall, I finally resumed my schooling.

Grandmother Elder died in 1954, and that essentially ended my visits to La Junta and with my dad. Other than the few letters we exchanged, I had less and less contact with him.

My stepdad adopted me in 1955, and my name legally changed to Kenneth Bledsoe. Again, this was a very confusing time for an 11-year-old boy. I couldn't understand how Vernon could allow my name to be changed. Didn't he love me anymore?

Luckily, I became involved in sports during middle school and high school, and my coaches helped channel my confusion, and sometimes anger, into football and track. I rarely saw Dad during these years, but occasionally, when I visited friends in Sterling, Colorado, I would stop by his house in La Junta. My relationship with my stepmother was never good, so these visits were often awkward. Dad and I, however, were always glad to see each other and tried hard to reconnect.

In 1963, I graduated from Highland High School in Albuquerque. My mom and stepdad hosted a reception at our house after the graduation ceremonies, and surprisingly, Vernon came. He didn't stay long, but just the fact he came meant a lot to me.

After graduation, I went to Fort Lewis College in Durango, Colorado where I received a bachelor's degree in history with an emphasis in education. I moved on to teach middle school history and physical education in Grants, New Mexico. There I met the love of my life, Phyllis, also a teacher, and we were married in 1969.

While continuing to teach in Grants, Phyllis and I sometimes talked about Vernon. She often encouraged me to reach out to him and schedule a time we could get together. So in February 1973, I wrote Vernon that our Spring Break would be in late March and asked if we could come see him. He and Phyllis had still not met. Vernon wrote back immediately saying that he

Chapter 6: Rattlesnake Bomber Base

would love to see us both.

Tragically, a few days before our scheduled visit, Vernon was killed in a single car accident on his way to work. His death left a terrible vacuum in my life. He would never meet my wife. He and I would never be able to sit as adults and talk about the things that mattered in our lives.

At his funeral, my aunts told Phyllis and me about Vernon's plane crash during WWII, and that he had pulled his best friend's body to shore. I felt intrigued by this story and vowed to someday discover details about the crash and the location of the wreckage. Then in the words of an Australian friend, I would 'walk in his steps.'

Vernon and Ken near Raton, NM
(Author's collection)

Grandmother Elder and Mildred, Vernon's sister
(Author's collection)

Echoes From an Eagle

Left to right: Grandmother Elder; Ken's cousin, George; Ken; Ken's cousins, Betty and Patricia
(Author's collection)

Vanessa Seekee, Royal Australian Army
(Courtesy of Vanessa Seekee)

The author, Vanessa, and Phyl in front of the Torres Strait Heritage Museum
(Author's collection)

CHAPTER 7

Australian Connection

I dedicated the time between Vernon's death and my retirement, to careers and family. Phyllis and I moved to Fort Collins, Colorado in 1976 where we both continued our careers in education, received master's degrees from Colorado State University, bought our first home, and started our family. Our daughter, Erin, was born in 1979, and with her birth, came mandatory visits to grandparents, themed birthday parties, dance lessons, sleepovers, and cheerleading.

Then in 2002 I retired. Since Phyllis still worked, this provided the perfect time to begin researching Vernon's WWII experiences. I read everything I could find that dealt with the fighting in Java and the Pacific Theater. I also reached out to the 19th BG Association hoping to find someone who might have served with Vernon.

But it wasn't until 2005 when Phyllis arranged Vernon's letters in chronological order that we identified the most important story to research. The letters talking about Houston Rice's death reminded us of the story my aunts told on the day Vernon was buried. Our mission, once again, shifted to determining the location of that crash and visiting it.

Seekee and Dietz

My first communication with Vanessa Seekee occurred in May of 2007. At that time, my search focused on the crashes of 19th Bomb Group planes that occurred in the Torres Strait region, north of Cape York, Australia. Two accidents in July of 1942, on and near Horn Island, were of particular interest. The date of the crashes coincided with the date of my father's accident in B-17 #655.

I first read about these accidents on Peter Dunn's *Oz at War* website, and contacted him.[1] Mr. Dunn was very helpful and recommended that I talk to Vanessa Seekee who lived on Horn Island. She authored *Horn Island: In Their Steps 1939-45*, a thorough history about the Australians and Americans who served on the island and fought together against the advancing Japanese forces in the Torres Strait.[2] Vanessa's book mentioned interviewing Ralph Dietz, a bottom turret gunner with the 93rd Squadron, who survived the crash of #655.

When the 19th returned to the U.S. in December of 1942, Ralph remained in Australia as an aircraft maintenance technician. He married his Australian sweetheart, Rae, and was later transferred stateside.

Ralph and Rae returned to Australia five times in the following years. On one of those trips, they visited Horn Island and were the guests of Vanessa and her husband, Liberty Seekee. Liberty, along with a friend, hired a small boat and took Ralph and Rae to the crash site of #655. The water was shallow enough at low tide that Dietz could see the wreckage of his B-17 bomber. Liberty's friend, Charles Snowden, dove down and retrieved a small piece from the wreckage and gave it to Ralph as a memento. When asked his reaction to being at the crash site again, Ralph said, "It was like a dream to see it [wreckage] again. When I saw it, I wondered how I got out of it."[3]

At 3:30 a.m. on July 14, the plane carrying the 21-year-old Dietz took off but failed to get enough lift under its wings.

> "...I knew we were in water when I saw a waterfall come through the bomb bay door. The lights went out. I couldn't feel any floor underneath or walls. I had been washed out of the plane. I just started swimming. I dropped my gun belts. I tried to get my jacket off but couldn't. I had no life pre-

Chapter 7: Australian Connection

server on. I swam for an hour. I was touching bottom with my toes when a boat picked us up."[4]

<u>NOTE</u>: Liberty took a picture of Ralph and Rae sitting in the boat above the wreckage of #655 with the shore line as a background. This picture would become key in my relocating the crash site 13 years later.

Ralph and Rae over the crash site (Photo by Liberty Seekee)

In Their Steps

After communicating with Vanessa, I found out that Ralph Dietz lived in Clarion, Pennsylvania; and she and her husband, Liberty, had visited him in the past. I immediately called information and located Ralph's phone number. With excitement I placed the call; and when he answered, I identified myself as the son of a fellow survivor of the crash.

Over the following weeks, Ralph and I became good friends. Our weekly phone conversations, numerous letters, and emails provided a clearer picture of the confusion and fear felt by the surviving crewmen that night.

Then in 2008, Phyllis and I flew out to Pennsylvania to meet

Ralph in person. Ralph's grandson, Mark, and his wife, Patti, were our gracious hosts. We will never forget the twinkle in Ralph's eye when we first met. He was in poor health, but was excited to tell his stories to a new audience.

During our stay in Pennsylvania, we heard a great deal about the crash. According to Dietz, there were mistakes in some of the written reports; and it was important to Ralph, since I was the son of one of the survivors, that he set me straight on what had really occurred that early morning off Horn Island. The most important detail that he wanted to correct was that, in some accounts, the identification of the two bombers that crashed that night was backwards. He insisted that it was B-17 #655, the one he was on, that crashed one mile off shore from Horn Island, and that it was piloted by Lt. Paul Lindsey. He said that B-17 #636, piloted by Lt. Curtis Holdridge, crashed into the soft mud just off the end of the runway on Horn Island. Ralph confirmed that three crewmen were killed in the crash of #655; and he stated that all the crew survived the Holdridge crash, though some were injured.

After spending two days with Ralph, we came away with an abiding respect for the man who had proudly served his country at a most difficult time. We were also impressed he could still recall events as though they happened yesterday. Before leaving, I promised Ralph to write the 'true story' detailing the crash of #655. He laughingly insisted that I finish the story before he 'passed on.' Sadly, he passed away in early 2010, four days before my mother. My search for 'official' records to corroborate Ralph's account of the crash continued.

Ken, Ralph and Phyllis at Ralph's home in Clarion, PA (Author's collection)

CHAPTER 8

'The Letter'

NOTE: My father and three others huddled in the radio room listening to the roar and feeling the vibration of a heaving bomber as it lumbered down the rain soaked runway, lit only by the flashes of lightening from a fierce tropical storm. A minute later he faced his greatest fear and at the same time lost his best friend.

I believed Vernon's letter to John Rice was key to learning more specifics about the crash of #655. What I could not glean from a newspaper headline or censored report, might be found in this letter. What would I have written to my best friend's father? How much information about the crash and Houston's death would Vernon give or want to give? John Rice was a strong man. Would Vernon have thought honesty and dignity to be the best approach? How would I have handled this sensitive task?
'The letter,' written nearly 67 years ago, might be faded yellow, torn, or possibly, discarded into a trash heap and burned. Certainly no copy was found in Vernon's shoe box of letters. If it still existed, how could I track this letter down? It was the proverbial, 'needle in a haystack' . . . no worse!

To my knowledge, the last known address of the Rice family was Ordway, Colorado, but I couldn't find a record of relatives currently living in Crowley County.

John W. Rice's letter written to Vernon in 1943 had a Richmond, California postmark, and he said he had three other sons that were in the service or would be soon – Lester at Camp Roberts, John Dean in the Navy, and Donald close to enlistment age.

No records, however, mentioned their living in Richmond today.

By utilizing the 1930 census for Colorado, I discovered Houston not only had three brothers, but also, a sister named Norma. Could one of John Rice's other sons or his daughter possibly still be alive?

My best chance of finding John's living relatives was to access Ancestry.com. I hadn't used the website in the past but thought it might help narrow my search. Surely, someone in the Rice family had become the recorder of their genealogy.

Navigating Ancestry.com was time consuming and frustrating, mainly due to my lack of experience. I hoped one of Houston's younger siblings, if living, knew something about 'the letter.' Maybe one of them even had it.

I discovered two of Houston's younger brothers had passed away . . . Lester Rice in 1990 and John Dean Rice in 1996. John Dean had lived in Middleton, Idaho, so I called the Rice families listed in the Middleton phone directory, but none were related. Some sounded rather gruff and didn't want to be bothered, but I did have a great discussion with one lady who seemed excited about my research and told me to let her know when I found out more. Her interest motivated me to continue my search.

Donald Rice and the younger sister, Norma, were now my only hope; but I soon exhausted all leads for finding Donald, the youngest brother. It was as though he had disappeared into thin air!

As I continued to seek information, the scope of possibilities began to narrow. At this point, I struggled to remain optimistic. Either I would find the one person who might know of 'the letter,' or my search would end permanently and with disappointment.

Norma Rice was only 13 in 1942 when her brother, Houston, died; and she lost her mother, Ona, two years earlier. No doubt she would have gone on with her life, gotten married, and raised her own family. Was it possible she had the family records, old letters, and pictures?

Chapter 8: 'The Letter'

I went back to searching on Ancestry.com for related family trees and discovered a living Rice in the Dougan Family Tree. Her name was Norma Rice Dougan, wife of Richard Dougan. The Dougan tree listed Norma's father as John W. Rice. Houston's younger sister . . . I was finally on to something! Her last known address was in Jena, Louisiana, and the current phone directory listed her address and phone number. Maybe the mystery would soon be solved.

Phyllis encouraged me to make the call . . . "What do you have to lose?" I called on a weekend in March of 2010. No one answered, and though I tried several more times, I got no answer. The following week, I sent Norma a letter explaining who I was and the relationship between her brother, Houston, and my father. I included my phone number, address, and email address.

I continued looking for other options in case I never heard from Norma. This search took me from Louisiana to North Dakota. Again, through Ancestry.com, I contacted Shirley Johnson, the niece of Norma's husband. Gracious and interested in my research, Shirley was very willing to contribute. She hoped her aunt could help, but said Norma suffered from Alzheimer's and had been in and out of the hospital over the last few weeks. However, Norma had a caretaker, Diane Paul, and Shirley promised to contact her regarding my search.

Norma's Alzheimer's discouraged me, and made me think that I might have reached a dead end. My mother had had Alzheimer's, and I knew firsthand, how the disease made it almost impossible to get reliable information in an interview. I began to question why this was so important to me? What's the point? But my need to read my father's words made it impossible to give up the search.

The Letter Exchange

Several weeks passed, and I continued to research other aspects of Vernon's combat experience, specifically, his being marooned on an island after a forced landing. When I opened my email one morning, I saw a message from Diane Paul, the caretaker of Norma Dougan. In her email, Diane reiterated that Norma's health was failing, and cautioned that her memory was unreliable.

Her next statement, however, was a stunner! Diane had contact information for two of Norma's nieces who might be of more help. Nieces!?? Donald Rice, the only remaining brother, was alive and in his eighties and had a daughter named Renee Wingerd. Sherry Baldridge, the other niece, was the daughter of a deceased sister I had not even known existed. Both women lived in California. Could this be the lead I'd been looking for all this time? Would either know anything about their uncle's crash or about their grandfather, John, receiving a letter from Vernon? I could barely control my excitement as I told Phyl about this new contact possibility. I decided to contact Renee first, hoping she could unlock the mystery of my dad's missing letter.

The next day, I called her; and though she was not there, her husband, Bill, took my message. When we made contact the following day, Renee and I immediately knew we had both made a prized discovery. I told Renee I had her grandfather's original letter to my father dated September 11, 1943, and I was holding it in my hand. In response she said, "Well, I have the original letter that your father sent my grandfather. It's pretty fragile and yellowed." I was ecstatic! Renee was the preserver and archivist of the Rice family history.

Ironically, all these years, we had both been researching the same events and looking for the letters written by my father and her grandfather. We enthusiastically agreed to exchange the original letters.

Renee and I, overwhelmed by what we had learned that morning, were excited to say the least. We immediately established a trusting, friendly rapport, bound together by the shared history of our loved ones. Renee recalled, as a small girl, going with

Chapter 8: 'The Letter'

her family to visit Houston's grave. He was interred at Golden Gate National Cemetery in May of 1949 when the Australian government returned his remains to the U.S. Too young to know her Uncle Houston, she, ironically, knew more specific details about the crash than I had previously found through research. I, in turn, knew more about the impact Houston's death had had on her grandfather.

Renee said that she had been unable to find anything in her grandfather's handwriting and would always cherish the letter I promised to send her. She also planned to make copies for the rest of her family.

I, on the other hand, would have a chance to read what must have been the most difficult letter Vernon had ever written. From 'the letter' I hoped to learn more about what actually happened that night, and possibly, more about the exact location of the crash. Most importantly, I wanted to see how Vernon had handled the difficult task of explaining to a father how his son had died. What would this reveal about Vernon's integrity as a man?

"He was my closest friend"

When we received Renee's packet in the mail, Phyllis and I sat down and carefully opened it. Sealed in a separate plastic sleeve, was a faded, yellow, two-page typed letter addressed to John W. Rice and signed Sgt. Elder. 'The letter' had been found! After eight years of searching, I now held it in my hands.

I couldn't read the words at first because of the tears in my eyes. So, I dug deeper in the packet and found two other letters. One was addressed to Otto Weiser, an Air Corp buddy who had been with Vernon and Houston at March Field. The letter to Otto expressed Vernon's grief over the loss of his friend, as well as, his need to find Mr. Rice:

Echoes From an Eagle

Dear Otto,
August 2, 1943

Boy I bet getting a letter from me is really going to be a surprise. Joe let me read the letter that he got from you yesterday, and it was sure swell to hear from you. Right now I'm *supposed* to be on duty here at the Bombsight shop but decided to….drop you a line. I'm section-chief of the dep't now so if any work comes up I'll let *my boys* do it. Nothing but a *big operator*. They're really keeping us busy around this damn place though and not a whole lot of time to loaf. Guess Joe told you about the field etc. so won't go into detail about this place. Guess it could be worse. In fact I've seen a lot worse places . . .

Guess you felt about as bad as I did about Rice being killed in that plane crash. Perhaps you would like to learn a little straight dope on it as I happened to be there too. We were taking off on a bombing mission from Horn Island, a small island at the northern tip of Australia. We had a bomb bay full of gas and a full load of bombs. Time of take-off was 3:30 A.M. and still dark . . . We got off the ground okay and about 200 ft. high, wheels up, and motors doing okay. We were indicating about 140 and about a mile off shore. For no apparent reason we started to go down. We really hit the water . . . Rice was by the ball turret and apparently was killed instantly as he had a bad looking place on his right temple . . . I got to go to his funeral. He was buried on Thursday Island which is a very small island about two miles from Horn Is. The ceremony was very simple but very nice considering where we were, and it was given by an Australian chaplain. I don't even like to think about Rice being gone but thought perhaps you might like to know about it. We sure had some good times together, and he's a guy I'll never forget. The last time Pat heard from his dad he said he was moving to someplace in Wash. or Oregon. He's not in Colorado anymore unless he

Chapter 8: 'The Letter'

came back. Sure wish I could get in touch with him as I have some pictures of Pat that was taken over there and know he would like to have.

What are you doing now anyway? How's about writing me a letter one of these days? That's all for this time but will try and write more often from now on.

Your Pal, Elder[1]

<u>NOTE</u>: *The 'Pat' mentioned in the letter to Otto referred to Houston's nickname, 'Patty' Rice.*

After reading Vernon's letter, Otto sent it to Doris Mae, the niece of Houston's father, and included Vernon's contact information at Pyote. As a result, Doris Mae mailed the Rice family's new address to Otto, and forwarded Vernon's letter to Mr. Rice. She included the following explanation with the letter:

August 20, 1943
Sand Springs, Okla.

Dear Uncle Johnny and Aunt Verna,
I'm sure you all have often heard Hustin speak of Otto Weiser his buddy in the army? Well I had a letter from him last wk. wanting to (know) how he could get in touch with Uncle Johnny – He said that a friend of his and Hustin had been with him when he was killed and he knew that you would want to know more about it. So I sent him your address but before he had time to get it he got a letter from this boy. He sent the letter for me to read and I'm going to send it on to you. I know after he gets your address he'll write you a much more sufficient one - I hope he can help you to know a little more about everything - and that what he has to tell you Uncle Johnny, can help ease your mind.
Love, Doris Mae[2]

NOTE: *Now I knew how Vernon had finally located Houston's family . . . another mystery solved.*

After receiving the new address for the Rice family, Vernon sent the following heartfelt letter to John Rice: (circa Sept. 4-6, 1943)

> T/Sgt. Vernon O. Elder
> 30th Bomb. Sqd. 19th Group
> Army Air Base Pyote, Texas
>
> Dear Mr. Rice
> I've intended to write you for quite some time, but had a little difficulty finding out your address.
> Perhaps one time or the other you have heard Houston speak of me as we were very close friends. We met back at March Field, California when our Squadron was stationed there and being that my home was in La Junta we used to talk about Colorado a great deal.
> I don't know much the Government told you about the accident that Houston was in but I'll try and give you a little more information on it as I happened to be with him at the time. I'm also sending you a few snapshots of him taken in our camp in Australia that I'm sure you would like to have.
> We left the States together leaving from Tampa, Florida in a Flying Fortress type airplane. Houston was the engineer and also took a position as one of the aerial gunners. Our first stop was Trinidad, British West Indies, from there to Belem, Brazil and we hopped off to Africa from Natal, Brazil. Our first stop in Africa was Accra which is on the Gold Coast of West Africa. We had two more stops there. One at Kano and the other at Khartaum. Our next stop was Cairo, Egypt then on to Karachi and Bangalore, India. We flew on to Sumatra, Dutch East Indies, took off soon afterwards for Java which is in the Dutch East Indies and this was our destination.

Chapter 8: 'The Letter'

We flew a lot of bombing missions in Java trying to stop the Japs from coming on down our way but with such very few airplanes we had and the air superiority of the Japs we were forced to evacuate to Australia. The small town we were at was Cloncurry in North Queensland. That's where those pictures were taken of Houston. One of them he is holding a baby Kangaroo we caught as a pet of ours. The other picture is myself, Jack Gardner and Houston.

One day in July we were ordered on a bombing mission. Houston wasn't flying on the crew I was on at that time but we were short a man so Houston volunteered to go with us on that mission. We took off and landed at Horn Island to re-fuel before going on to New Guinea. Horn is a very small island at the northern tip of Australia. We landed in the evening and takeoff time was 3:30 A.M. the morning of the 12th I believe. We took off okay but when we were about a mile out over the ocean the plane started to lose altitude. Why, we never found out, but we crashed in the ocean. One thing I'm sure and that's that Houston never suffered in the least because it all happened so fast. He was already dead when he was taken ashore and examined by an Australian doctor. The only mark he had on him was on the head by the temple. His face still had that pleasant, smiling look that all the fellows got to know so well. He was one of the best thought of guys in the squadron, everyone liked him. He was especially thought of in the squadron because of his ability as a good engineer and gunner and his willingness to do his part whatever the job might be.

I went to his funeral and don't know if the Gov't told you where he was buried or not, but I will tell you a little about it. He was buried on Thursday Island which is another small island right next to Horn Is. It's a small but beautiful little island very tropical looking covered with palm trees and green trees and bushes. An Australian Chaplain gave the service; and all though it was a simple ceremony, under the conditions, it was nicest a person could ask for. A lot of Australian officers and men were present along with a few of us American boys. I know it was a great loss to you, Mr. Rice, as it was for me because he was my closest friend.

I hope what little I've told you will be a help and somewhat of a relief to you and if there is anything else I can tell you that you might like to know I'd be more than glad to.

Sincerely,
Sgt. Elder[3]

<u>NOTE</u>: *Vernon's letter gave detailed descriptions of the crash—including the time and place—and of Houston's burial ceremony on Thursday Island. For Houston's father, this was another step toward closure. For me, the letter confirmed Ralph Dietz's account of the crash location and set the stage for our long journey.*

9
CHAPTER

Adventure 'Down Under'

NOTE: There was no doubt in my mind that the wreckage of my father's B-17 bomber was a mile out from the northern coast of Horn Island, and I was determined to find it!

The time came to plan our great adventure! Phyl and I had always wanted to see Australia, and now we had an exciting reason to go. We contacted Vanessa Seekee expressing our desire to visit Horn Island and to see the wreckage of #655. She responded the next day saying the dry season just began, and that she would book our accommodations at her resort to coincide with the reunion of the Australian 34th Heavy Antiaircraft Battery, the unit assigned to protect both Australian and American facilities and aircraft on Horn Island. WWII veterans, Gordon Cameron and Gerry Merrett, who served as young gunners, planned to be there along with their family members, friends, and other Australians interested in the war history of Horn Island. Vanessa would also arrange for a boat to take us to the crash site. We would be the first Americans to visit the location since Ralph and Rae Dietz. After a 10 year search for the crash site of my father's B-17, I was finally going to see it.

In June 2010, we booked our flight to Australia, and in September, embarked on our long journey. We flew from Denver to Los Angeles; and from LAX, our Qantas flight crossed the Equator and the International Date Line, arriving in Sydney 15 hours later.

Australia is the only continent that is also a country, a big country, comparable in size of land area to the continental U.S. It has a population of 24 million people concentrated mostly along the coastal areas. Eighty percent of the plants and animals that live in Australia can't be found anywhere else in the world. Of the world's 10 most poisonous snakes, all are indigenous to Australia.[1] As one of our Aussie friends told us, everything there either wants to sting you, bite you, or eat you!

We spent four days in Sydney where we visited the Opera House, took a harbor cruise, and saw the Anzac Museum, as well as, the botanical gardens. We then headed north to Cairns (pronounced "cans"), an important city in the history of the 19th BG. After the crash of #655, the crew members received a pass and went to a city (Cairns) with bright lights, dancing, and very nice people. Cairns was where they were sent to rest and recuperate, essential in maintaining the health and morale of the airmen. It's where we began to retrace Vernon's steps.

However, the first thing we did in Cairns was take a catamaran cruise to the Great Barrier Reef, about 25 miles out from the coast. Although we saw only a tiny speck of this 1300 mile reef, it lived up to its reputation as a true wonder of the world!

The next day, we rode the narrow gauge train from Cairns to Kuranda, located on the Atherton Plateau. This train was used during WWII to transport goods and troops to the Mareeba Air Base. From Kuranda, we took the Sky Rail over the rain forest and the spectacular Barron River Gorge. This gave us a bird's eye view of the rugged area and helped us understand the challenges our American airmen faced while living there in tents. It also explained why the Japanese never located the base at Mareeba.

In His Steps at Mareeba Air Base

Before leaving for Australia, I contacted Damian Waters, the author of *Beau's, Butchers, & Boomerangs*, a historical account of the Mareeba Air Field.[2] I told him of our impending trip, and that we planned to visit Mareeba. He offered to take us on a tour

Chapter 9: Adventure 'Down Under'

of the area and to show us what remains of the airfield (known today as Hoevet Field). We jumped at the opportunity.

Therefore, the day after our visit to Kuranda, we caught an early bus from Cairns to Mareeba where we met Damian. He graciously committed the day to our first-rate tour of the area so essential to the Allies during the war. This strategic airfield served as a staging base for American and Australian missions against enemy targets throughout New Guinea and island bases in the Coral Sea. The quiet tranquility we experienced was nothing like those days many years earlier when the ground shook with the roar of Allied bombers taking off for dangerous and often deadly missions. Reinforced cement ammunition bunkers stood deserted. Posted signs outside the entrances warned to watch where you stepped, lest you disrupt the sleep of the resident poisonous snakes. We walked on the remains of one of the original runways, still intact and recognizable. A local farmer bought this land after the war, and left the ageing runway surface to serve as his driveway. Another of the main runways used during the war, still serves small aircraft flying in and out of Mareeba.

Damian Waters and Phyl standing on airstrip
(Author's collection)

Farmer's huge driveway
(Author's collection)

Mounted on a stone wall at the Mareeba Airfield is a B-17 propeller and below it, a plaque is dedicated to both the Royal Australian Air Force and the United States Army Air Corps' 19th and 43rd Bomber Groups.

". . . Mareeba Airfield played an important role in the defense of Australia and in turning the tide of the war in the SW Pacific. Mareeba was the home for hundreds of young Australian and American Air Force personnel, many of whom made the ultimate sacrifice."[3]

Chapter 9: Adventure 'Down Under'

<u>NOTE</u>: As we toured Mareeba with Damian, we were struck by the feeling that the spirits of all those brave men were with us.

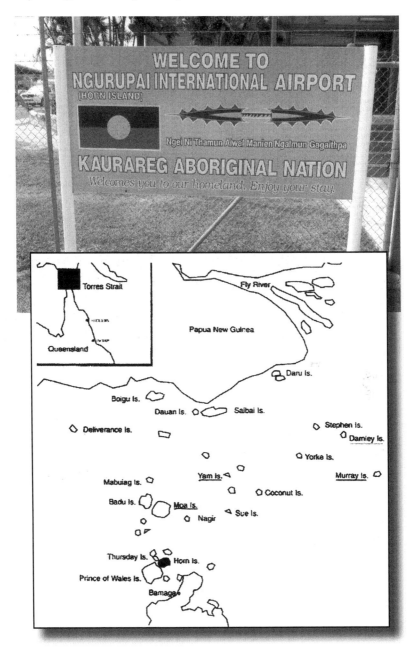

Ngurupai (Horn Island)

The day after our Mareeba visit, we flew on a Qantas turboprop from Cairns to our final destination of Ngurapai (Horn Island), located in the Torres Strait, 10 degrees south of the Equator. We flew virtually the same flight pattern young Australian and American airmen followed on their way to bomb Japanese airbases and naval facilities. Our flight took a little more than an hour as compared to the two hour journey in the B-17s in 1942. Flying north over Cape York, Australia, we covered more than 1034 kilometers of vast, sparsely populated landscape. Below, one could see the unpaved highway that stretched from Laura to Bamaga, located at what the Aussies call 'the top.'

There are two seasons in the Torres Strait . . . wet and dry. For eight months a year, the low, scrubby bushland on Horn Island is dry and can hardly be called a tropical island. Horn Island has no natural water source, so a large dam was built to store the rainwater that falls during the rainy season. It is home to stubborn green ants, little geckoes, and crocodiles called 'salties.' Crocodile warning signs are posted throughout the region.

In preparation to land, our plane crossed over Horn Island and approached the small airport from the west. We landed on the same runway my father's planes used on their return from WWII bombing missions. It all seemed surreal!

American Armed Forces first constructed the Ngurupai Airport during the war, and only a very small terminal remains. Within minutes after deplaning, a cart loaded with luggage pulled up to the front door of the terminal, and passengers calmly located their own bags. There was no rushing around to catch connecting flights, since the only ones leaving were small carriers that made short hops to other Torres Strait Islands; and these flights pretty much worked on 'island time.' It was great!

Vanessa Seekee arrived in a bus from her resort; and we, along with other guests, soon drove down the only paved road on the island, headed to the small community of Wasaga, home to the

Chapter 9: Adventure 'Down Under'

majority of the islanders. Our accommodations were excellent at the Gateway Torres Strait Resort, owned and operated by Vanessa and Liberty Seekee. They had everything we needed . . . two meals a day and a bar!

Our visit to Horn Island was timed to coincide with the reunion of the 34th Australian Heavy Antiaircraft Battery. During the war, the 34th protected the Australian and American installations at the island air base. This far northern outpost was all that stood between the advancing Japanese and Australia's mainland, however, these men are known as 'the Forgotten Army.'[4] Most Australians never knew about the 34th or their service on Horn Island, just as most Americans didn't know that the 19th Bomb Group flew out of this part of Australia.

The 26 Australians attending the reunion were family members and friends of 34th veterans who served on Horn Island. Gordon Cameron and Gerry Merrett were the only veterans in attendance. Gerry shared with us that he joined the army at age 15! Major Mark Prideaux of the Royal Australian Army also joined the group. He was the acting Deputy Director of Indigenous Affairs in Australia. Despite being the only Americans, Phyllis and I were drawn to these Aussies by the shared experience of having relatives who fought together to defend Australia and Horn Island.

Over the next six days, in a landscape wholly unfamiliar to us, we walked the overgrown, narrow trails that led us to slit trenches, wreckages of planes and antiaircraft bunkers scattered throughout the island. These bunkers were once manned by young Australian, Filipino, and Torres Strait islanders, determined to stand their ground, no matter what the Japanese threw at them.

Slit trench in the bush
(Author's collection)

Warning sign; It got our attention!

Beer bottles lie today where they were discarded 1942-43
(Author's collection)

Plane wreckage today on Horn Island
(Author's collection)

Chapter 9: Adventure 'Down Under'

The Torres Strait Islanders

Torres Strait is named for a Spanish captain who sailed through the region in 1606 on his way to the Philippines. Evidence of human settlement in the region dates back 2500 years. The islanders are culturally and genetically Melanesian people, as are the people of Papua New Guinea. They are different from the Aboriginal people of Australia. Today there are 6800 islanders who live in the area of Torres Strait; and 42,000 others live outside of this area, mostly in North Queensland.

The indigenous people of the Torres Strait have distinct cultures which vary slightly from island to island. They are seafaring people, and engage in trade with people of Papua New Guinea and Australia.[5] Like those of neighboring Papua, the islanders are agriculturalists but supplement their food supplies through hunting and gathering. Turtle, crayfish, crabs, shellfish, reef fish, wild fruits, and vegetables are all traditional parts of their diet. The language spoken depends on the regional location of the many islands. The Australian Aboriginal language and languages spoken in Papua New Guinea are the most common, though, English is widely spoken on Horn and Thursday Island.

Thursday Island is located three miles west of Horn Island. It is the Administrative capital of the Torres Strait Islands and the base for the Australian Joint Defense Facility (JDF) which includes C Company of the Far North Queensland Regiment.

Approximately 30 percent of this unit is composed of Torres Strait indigenous soldiers and mainland aborigines. Its diverse composition gives it a unique character.[6] The soldiers are permitted by the Royal Australian Army to do drills that replicate their ancestral dances, accompanied by the playing of drums and didgeridoos. These drills are a fascinating example of maintaining military discipline, while at the same time, preserving the cultural identity of the soldiers. Many of the soldiers in C Company had a father or grandfather who served in the army in

WWII, however, most of these veterans never received medals or recognition for their service. Australia is still trying to right these wrongs.

C Company, Royal Australian Army, (Author's collection)

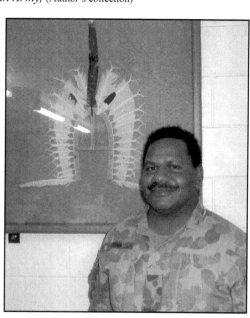

Morris Nona is from Badu Island.

Torres Strait symbol on flag; Headdress represents the Torres Strait Island people.
(Author's collection)

Chapter 9: Adventure 'Down Under'

Royal Australian Army vets Gordon and Gerry singing Thursday Island song. (Author's collection)

Sarpeye: A Dinner to Remember

One of the highlights of our journey to the Torres Strait was an invitation to attend a formal dinner at the Australian military base on Thursday Island. We rode the ferry, the island kids' school bus, over from Horn Island. The event honored the 34th Antiaircraft Battery of the Royal Australian Army. The guests of honor were the two Australian WWII veterans, Gordon Cameron and Gerry Merrett. The base commander, Major Lane, presented each man a plaque giving long overdue credit for their service to Australia.

The dinner guests included the indigenous members of Company C, who had previously never been invited to dine with the officers. The seating was arranged to alternate indigenous guests with family members of the 34th Battery. Phyllis sat next to First Sergeant Lewis, of aboriginal descent, and I sat next to trooper Morris Nona of Badu Island. Morris mentioned he had never seen snow, so a couple of months later, I mailed snow scenes from our home in Colorado. Being the only Americans in attendance, we were something of a curiosity to the indigenous soldiers. Our accents were strange and made them laugh!

Behind the dais hung a picture of Queen Elizabeth II. We all rose to commence the dinner with a toast to "The Queen." Phyllis and I had never toasted a queen before, and there were many more toasts to follow. We were truly far from home and enjoying every second!

Midway through the dinner, I was invited to speak. On this momentous occasion where the indigenous soldiers could dine with their officers, I felt it appropriate to share the challenges faced by the Navajo Code Talkers during WWII. Their language and cultural differences often made it hard for them to obey military rules and regulations. For example, a Marine drill sergeant, when giving orders, expected a recruit to make eye contact, which was considered bad manners to a Navajo. These cultural snags made it difficult for a Navajo soldier to fit in or be accepted, but both sides had to find a way to overcome their differences. The unique Navajo language became a secret weapon for the American forces fighting in the Pacific Theater. The Navajo Code Talkers created the only code for communication never broken by the Japanese. The huge tactical and strategic advantage this code provided the Allies was much more important than whether a soldier made eye contact with an officer.

The soldiers present were curious as to why two Americans had come so far to reach an island unknown to most Australians. I explained that after years of research, we had come half way around the world to find the crash site of my father's WWII bomber. Our long journey would end in the Torres Strait, about a mile out from Horn Island. I shared my dream to reach the location and dive down to see what remained of the wreckage after 68 years in the ocean.

Australians have never forgotten the role Americans played in the defense of their country, and the hospitality demonstrated at the dinner was heartwarming. They included us in the ceremo-

Chapter 9: Adventure 'Down Under'

nies that honored Mr. Cameron and Mr. Merrett, and we had the privilege to watch our friend, Vanessa Seekee, receive her Commission in the Royal Australian Army. Also, for the first time, the indigenous Australians, whose contributions to the war effort had been long forgotten, were included in the tributes.

On our arrival back at Horn Island, we said our goodbyes to our new Aussie friends. We all knew that we probably would never see each other again. Early the next morning, Phyllis and I were scheduled to go out to the crash site of Vernon's plane, and they would be leaving the island. We had been brought together by a common bond forged by the war experiences of our relatives who served, fought, and died together in and around Torres Strait. Lest we forget!

Gordon Cameron reading dedication at an antiaircraft bunker on Horn island.
(Author's collection)

Gordon Cameron and Ken
(Author's collection)

Gerry Merrett and Ken
(Author's collection)

*Major Mark Prideaux,
Deputy Director
of Indigenous Affairs*
(Author's collection)

10
CHAPTER

Long Ago, But Not Forgotten

Ten years ago, Phyllis and I read the letters written by my father in 1942. They chronicled the events from the most traumatic year of his life when he flew combat missions in the SW Pacific. One letter described ". . . an experience I'll never forget." His B-17 bomber crashed into the Torres Strait killing three of the crewmen, one of whom was his best friend. Several of the ensuing letters talked about how much this crash affected him. So finding the location where my dad's life changed forever became my goal.

After all the years of poring through letters, documents, maps, and interviewing a survivor of the crash, the day had finally arrived. I was on Horn Island and would attempt to locate the wreckage. I hoped to dive down to see the remains of the bomber. Since local fishing laws restricted scuba diving near the surrounding coral reefs, I only had snorkel gear (minus the flippers) and a Kodak underwater camera.

Liberty Seekee arranged for two local fishermen, Sam Salee from Papua New Guinea and Eddie Mau from Queensland, to take the three of us to the general area of the crash. We were told to meet Sam and Eddy at the small wharf in Wasaga at 7 a.m. However, Sam attended a family funeral and didn't arrived until 11:00. By that time, the wind and rising tide were concerning, and could possibly make spotting the plane much more difficult. It didn't matter. Phyl and I had come too far not to give it a go!

After Sam's arrival in his small fishing boat, we headed east from Wasaga and about a mile north of Horn Island. Although Sam and Eddie were familiar with the submerged coral reefs off Horn Island, it had been awhile since they had fished in our target area. They couldn't guarantee finding the wreckage, given the increasing wind, rising tide, and murky water. We only knew its relative location based on information in my father's letters and a picture taken 13 years earlier of Ralph Dietz

Eddie Mau, the optimist — (taken by Ken)

and his wife Rae. The coastal background in their picture would guide us, both in alignment and distance from shore.

Eddie was spotting from the bow of the boat, and after about 30 minutes, signaled that we were over the crash site. I was already in the water when Liberty told Phyl that 'salties' had been spotted in the area a few days earlier. (Getting bit or stung was one thing, but to be eaten by anything would ruin the whole day!) He grabbed his fishing spear and followed me down. The wreckage was supposed to be lying partly on a coral reef at a depth of 8 to 25 feet. Liberty and I split up, stayed within about 20 yards of each other, but found no sign of wreckage.

Liberty and I searching for the wreckage. Eddie spotting — (taken by Phyl)

After a disappointing 20 min-

Chapter 10: Long Ago, But Not Forgotten

ute search, Liberty and I got back in the boat. This time, Sam did the spotting while Eddie took over the steering. Sam directed him to move the boat toward a large coral reef about 60 meters away. We scanned the water for any sign of the wreckage. I looked at Phyl and thought, we have come so far and are so close; what if we never find the bomber?

Then Sam pointed his finger straight up, looked back with a smile, and pointed down. He had spotted the wreckage of Flying Fortress #655. It took only about 10 seconds to put on my snorkel gear; and Sam threw out the anchor. Then Liberty and I were over the side and into the water. With the Kodak camera looped around my wrist, I grabbed the anchor chain with both hands and pulled myself down.

After so many years in the ocean, the coral and sea plants covering the skeletal remains of the plane waved quietly with the current. I took a few pictures then handed the camera to Liberty because he wanted to swim down deeper. A decade of work brought me to this moment. Looking at the wreckage, I could now better understand why Ralph Dietz and Vernon felt lucky to get out alive. Finally, I was walking, or rather swimming, in their steps.

Above: Sam spotting the wreckage.
Left: Anchor chain near wreckage — (taken by Ken)

111

Echoes From an Eagle

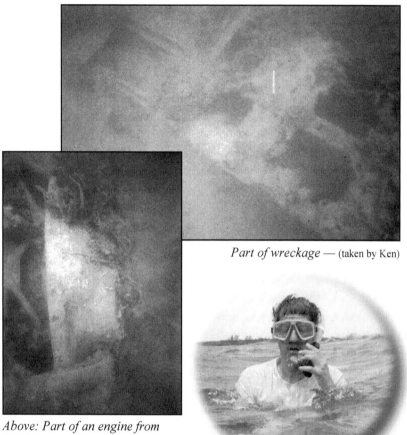

Part of wreckage — (taken by Ken)

Above: Part of an engine from #655 — (taken by Ken)

Above: Okay, I had no flippers, the wreckage was 8'-25' down, and there had been recent 'saltie' (salt water croc) sightings. No worries! Just hold my breath and take pictures.
— (taken by Phyl)

Left: Flag from Vernon's grave; Fort Logan National Cemetery —
(taken by Liberty)

Chapter 10: Long Ago, But Not Forgotten

Thirty minutes later, Liberty and I crawled back in the boat, tired and quietly reflecting on what we had seen. Diving down to see the wreckage had been an experience I would never forget. As she helped me back into the boat, Phyl's expression revealed relief and a sense of closure. As we slowly pulled away from B-17 #655, we felt the presence of the brave men who struggled to survive that long ago night. Words can't express the full measure of their courage, sacrifice, and will to live. We will always honor them and those who followed in their steps.

<u>NOTE</u>: *While Liberty and I were in the water, Eddy and Sam asked Phyl questions about the crash and the crew on board that stormy night. They listened to the story, but at the same time, kept a watchful eye on us in the water. Knowing Sam and Eddie often dove in these waters for crawfish and that Liberty had been raised and taught to swim in the area, prevented Phyl from being overly concerned about my safety. She did, however, admit her relief when we were back in the boat and headed back to the dock*

Echoes from the Past

The next day, we said our goodbyes to Liberty, Vanessa and other Torres Strait and Australian friends. Without the Seekees' assistance, encouragement, and guidance, we would never have been able to accomplish our mission.

Later that afternoon, Vanessa drove us to the small airport on Horn Island. While waiting to board, we sat on a small patio not far from our plane and reflected on the experiences we shared during our six day stay in the Torres Strait. As our flight time approached, I looked through our boarding passes for the flight back to Cairns, and from there on to Brisbane. Phyl and Vanessa were surprised when I started laughing and asked me to share the joke. I handed them our boarding passes from Cairns to Brisbane and told them to look at the flight number. It was Qantas Flight #655. How ironic! Vanessa said we were truly "walking in their steps." Was the crew of B-17 #655 trying to let us know they had been watching?

Finding the wreckage of #655 had been accomplished, and with that, a sense of closure. As we lifted off the same runway so many American and Australian flyers used 68 years earlier, our plane banked to the north and flew just a mile off the northern coast giving us one last look at the blue-green waters off Horn Island, the final resting place of Flying Fortress #655.

Summary

In the opening days of World War II, the young flyers of the 19th Bomb Group faced an immediate challenge. The early months of 1942 clearly favored the advancing forces of the Japanese. In the Philippines, the ground personnel of the 19th joined the infantry units in fighting the invaders. Some were evacuated, some escaped, but most were either killed or captured.

By moving to Java, the 19th, along with the Royal Australian Air Force and the Dutch, were the first airmen to initiate offensive bombing missions against the Japanese in Sumatra, Java, Borneo, and later, the SW Pacific over northern New Guinea, New Britain, and the Solomons. Newly trained B-17 crews arrived from the U.S. They were angered and anxious to strike back at the Japanese military forces, though that would be more of a hope than a reality.

With the subsequent loss of these regions to the Japanese, the defense of Northern Australia became the primary mission of the Royal Australian Army, Navy, and Air Force, as well as, the American flyers of the 19th BG. The logistical challenges of flying long distances over water; the unpredictable, fierce tropical storms; and the difficulties of getting supplies and equipment from the distant United States, posed an uphill fight. On far too many occasions the B-17s were called upon to commit themselves to actions at the extreme edge of their endurance.

Foremost, was the challenge of flying in a tropical environment where storms of ferocious violence caused more dread than the dangerous missions the airmen flew, in fact, more B-17s were lost to weather than from enemy action. The alternating heat and rain brought mud and dust in turn, and made servicing the planes a nightmare. On most missions the B-17s were forced to go into action in very small numbers. For a squadron to be at 50 percent strength (five or more aircraft) was little short of miraculous. Military historian, H. P. Willmott summarized,

"... the overall Pacific experience was an unfortunate one for the B-17 and its crews, because the odds were heavily stacked against it from the start."[1]

Despite the challenges, the brave men of the 19th Bomb Group answered their call to duty. They were the "tip of the sword" for the Army Air Corp's offensive operations against the Japanese in the SW Pacific. They defended the Torres Straits, the northern gateway to Australia, by striking Japanese bases with every bomber deemed combat-worthy. By the end of 1942, over 5000 Australian and American servicemen devoted themselves to this goal. They would not be defeated! With the power and strength provided by the American industrial output of military equipment, coupled with the gradual weakening of Japanese forces in the region, the defense of Australia was finally realized.

After nearly a year, the battle tested and weary 19th BG was sent back to the U.S. and assigned to the 'Rattlesnake' Bomber Base in Pyote, Texas. They had seen more than their share of challenges during the early and critical months of the war, and their experience and skills would be of great value in training others for strategic and aerial combat in the battles still to be fought. Many of the 19th BG's personnel were assigned to Great Bend, Kansas to train in the Air Corp's newest bomber, the B-29, which would carry them to the heart of Japan.

Technical Sgt. Vernon Elder finished the war at 'Rattlesnake' Bomber Base as a section chief for security at the Norden bombsight building. He was soon holding his baby son, who 66 years later dove on the wreckage of B-17 #655, where Vernon had lost his best friend and was forever changed.

<u>NOTE</u>: *Because of the hectic year that the 19th BG spent in the SW Pacific, few official reports were ever written. Those that did exist were either lost or destroyed in a fire in St. Louis, Missouri, after the war. Most information about this historic bomb group came from primary sources – letters, diaries, scrapbooks, and photos – provided by the airmen themselves.*

Epilogue

The Cappelletti-Lindsey Connection

After returning from Australia, I continued my search for 'official' records to corroborate Vernon's and Ralph Dietz's accounts of the crash of #655. In 2011, as part of this search, I sent an inquiry to The Royal Gorge Regional & History Center in Canon City, Colorado for information regarding Lt. Paul Lindsey. One of the newspaper articles I received reported on Paul's death on August 16, 1942, during a flare test in Australia.

Since Paul was considered the hometown hero, the community decided to raise $300,000 to purchase a bomber, "Royal Gorge No. 1," in his memory. A crowd of 850 people, including Miss Billie Lou Lindsey, Paul's younger sister, turned out for a program at the local high school gym. One of the speakers was Lt. Frank Cappelletti, a navigator with the 19th BG. Cappelletti told the hushed crowd:

> "Only the fact that my birthday fell on August 16th kept me from dying with Lt. Lindsey that night . . . I had gone into town to celebrate by going to a show when Paul took off to test a new type of flares.
>
> People on shore saw his four-motored bomber catch fire. He tried to make land, did circle town and could have landed. But it would have meant death to those in the town and he circled back out to sea. His ship crashed 300 yards off shore, and as it did there was an explosion. It sank immediately.
>
> In Paul Lindsey, Canon City has a hero of which you can be proud . . ."[1]

After reading this article, I wondered whether Frank Cappelletti could still be alive. I found a telephone number for him in Tampa, Florida, placed the call, but had to leave a message. To my surprise, it was his widow, Rose, who returned my call. She expressed interest and excitement in my research and offered to share Frank's papers, scrapbook, and photos. In fact, she mailed them to me asking only that I "treat them with the reverence they deserved and that I return them once I'd copied what I needed."[2]

Feeling humbled and privileged to be entrusted with Frank's memoirs, I waited anxiously for the delivery of Rose's "holy grail." When the package arrived, I quickly realized it was a treasure trove of information about the 19th, all from primary sources.

Of special interest, was the summary Frank composed in late 1942, prior to the 19th BG's return to the U.S. In it, he documented each plane destroyed or operated in Australia. One of his detailed accounts was for the crash of B-17s #636 and #655. It stated that #636, piloted by Lt. Holdridge with Lt. Perkins as his navigator, crashed at Horn Island, with all crew safe. Flight #655, with Lt. Paul Lindsey as pilot and Sgt. Houchins as bombardier, crashed in the ocean one mile out from Horn Island with the loss of three crewmen, including Houchins.

Since Cappelletti flew on most of the B-17s in Australia, and as an officer, knew the pilots, I believed this report to be as close as I would ever come to official documentation of what happened off Horn Island the morning of July 14, 1942. In

Picture courtesy of Rose Cappelletti, wife of the Colonel

Epilogue

my mind, Ralph's and Vernon's accounts of the crash had finally been vindicated.

<u>NOTE</u>: *After the war and 91 missions later, Lt. Frank Cappelletti completed a distinguished career in the Air Force attaining the rank of 'Full Bird' Colonel. He was instrumental in developing new navigation systems for the 'Strategic Air Command,' participated in the atomic tests in the Pacific in the 1950's, and served in Vietnam. He was also a Russian translator in both a military and civilian capacity. On one occasion, he was called a hero and replied, "The real heroes never came home." Cappelletti took "eternal flight" in 2007.*

The Lindsey Reunion — 2012

Through Ancestry.com I found Tony Maine, a descendant in the Lindsey Family Tree, and emailed him during the spring of 2012. I told Tony about the information I had accumulated regarding his relative, Paul Lindsey. He in turn contacted Keith Lindsey, a nephew of Paul. As a result, Keith invited Phyllis and me to the annual Lindsey reunion. So in August, we flew to California to meet the Lindsey family.

In all, there were about 30 family members present, most of whom had heard about Paul Lindsey's heroics in Java which led to his receiving the Distinguished Flying Cross. However, they were interested in learning more details about their hero's WWII experiences. The family had rarely discussed Paul or his death, because when he was reported missing-in-action, his parents were so grief stricken that they were reluctant to discuss any of the details with Paul's siblings. Therefore, they knew almost nothing about his crash off Horn Island, Australia in July of 1942 or about his fatal crash a month later.

Having done research on both of the crashes, as well as, having done a dive on the wreckage off Horn Island, I prepared a power point presentation including Lindsey's July crash of B-17 #655. I explained that my father, Sgt. Vernon Elder, Lindsey's tail gunner, was in this crash. The presentation gave a step-by-step description of the events that occurred on the early morning off Horn Island, Australia. It explained that, though slightly injured, Paul and my dad kept the body of a fellow Coloradoan afloat until an Australian crash boat picked them up over an hour later. My talk, also, provided a detailed description of how Paul died in the flare test tragedy, and included Cappelletti's account of the crash.

My father had a deep respect for Paul. Not only did they share a sense of duty to their country, but also the love of their home state of Colorado. The descendants of the Lindsey family had always wondered about their Uncle Paul, and my research about Vernon's WWII experiences brought us together, not by accident, but through a shared history. As one of the Lindsey descendants told me later, my talk provided a sense of closure because many of the questions she had carried for years were finally answered. It was gratifying to share what I'd learned about their heroic uncle, and I think Vernon would have been proud that I reached out to the family of one of the 'Colorado Connection.'

Echoes From an Eagle

I spent hundreds of hours reading my father's letters, searching for clues about his thoughts, feelings, and fears. What I realized about Vernon through the letters and my visits with him, was that he came home wounded, not by bullets or shrapnel but by jaundice and the emotional damage suffered due to the dangerous missions flown and the dread and terror experienced during aerial combat. Gone were the innocence and naivety this small town boy once possessed. He never bragged or lingered on his role as a B-17 gunner, but it was obvious the crashes he survived and the loss of two close friends, Houston Rice and Paul Lindsey, haunted him the rest of his life.

Upon his return from overseas, Vernon wrote a letter to the father of Houston Rice, who died in the crash of #655. In several letter's home, he also expressed his sadness and sympathy at the loss of his other friend, Lt. Paul Lindsey. Their 'Colorado Connection' led them to fly many missions together, always watching each other's back. Vernon was the only one of the three to come home, and he never recovered from their loss.

His marriage to my mother and his first job as a civilian in California were both short. Vernon then retreated to his hometown, La Junta, Colorado, where his widowed mother, older siblings, school friends, and fellow Koshare Boy Scout troop members provided a screen of security from the memories of combat and war. He returned to the things that he loved and needed for healing . . . solitude, nature, and wandering the sand hills and prairies of southeast Colorado, occasionally, taking me along to hunt arrowheads.

Sporadically, I went to visit Vernon. He was quiet and often seemed nervous, but always had a smile for me and his friends around town. I never once saw him show anger or bitterness. To me, he was a gentle soul who only wanted peace.

I have often wondered what Vernon would have thought about

this story. No doubt I would have heard something like, "Well it wasn't quite like that," or possibly, "It was more terrifying than you can imagine." A line from one of his letters said it all ". . . I've had enough thrills to last me a lifetime." His premature death left only his letters as a legacy. By writing this story, I tried to reconnect with my dad and discover the experiences that shaped his life. My biggest regret is that I never heard the story told in his own words. He is gone, but not forgotten.

Bibliography

Books

Alexander, Thomas E. *Rattlesnake Bomber Base*. Abilene, Texas: State House Press, 2005.

Ancestry.com; Lindsey genealogy, 2010.

Bartsch, William H. *Every Day A Nightmare*, College Station, Texas: Texas A&M University Press, 2010.

Birdsall, Steve. *Flying Buccaneers: The Illustrated Story of Kenney's Fifth Air Force*. Garden City, New York: Doubleday, 1977.

Bryson, Bill. *In a Sunburned Country*. Broadway Books, 2000.

Bowman, Martin. *B-17 Flying Fortress Units of the Pacific War*. Botley Oxford: Osprey, 2003.

Bowman, Martin. *B-17 Combat Missions.* London: Elephant Book Company, 2007.

Brokaw, Tom. *The Greatest Generation*. New York: Dell Publishing, 2001.

Carson, Lt. Col. Eugene (Ret). *Wing Ding-Memories of a Tail Gunner*. United States of America: Xlibris Corporation, 2000.

Edmonds, Walter D. *They Fought With What They Had*. Boston: Little Brown and Company, 1951.

Darnell, Doris Lindsey. *Memoirs*. Reno, Nevada: Frandsen Humanities Press, 2001.

Dunn, Peter. *Australia at War*. 5th Air Force USAAF in Australia during WWII. 2015.

Freeman, Roger A. *B-17 Fortress at War*. London: Ian Allan LTD. 1977.

Freeman, Roger A. *The B-17 Flying Fortress Story*. New York: Sterling Publishing Co., 1998.

Gamble, Bruce. *Fortress Rabaul*. Minneapolis, MN: Zenith Press, 2010.

Hardison, Priscilla. *The Suzy-Q*. with Anne Wormser. Boston: Houghton Mifflin Co., 1943.

Harrison, Richard Edes. *Mercator Projection of S.W. Asia*. 1942.

Haugland, Vern. *The AAF Against Japan*. New York: Harper and Brothers, 1948.

Jablonski, Edward. *Flying Fortress*. New York: Doubleday and Company, 1965.

Kenney, George C. *General Kenney Reports*. New York: Duell, Sloan, and Pearce, 1949.

Mingos, Howard. *American Heroes of the War in the Air*. New York: Lanciar Publishers, Inc, 1943.

Mitchell, John H. *In Alis Vicimus, On Wings We Conquer.* Springfield, MO: G.E.M. Publishers, 1990.

Bibliography

Morison, Samuel Eliot. *The Two Ocean War*. New York: Little, Brown and Company, 1963.

Nielsen, Peter. *Diary of WWII North Queensland*. Smithfield, QLD: Nielsen Publishing, 1993.

Rorrison, James D. *Nor the Years Contemn: Air War On The Australian Front 1941 – 42*. Hamilton Central, Q. James Ferguson PTY LTD, 1992.

Salecker, Gene Eric. *Fortress Against the Sun*. United States of America: De Capo Press, 2001.

Sinton, Russell L. *The Menace from Moresby*. San Angelo, Texas: Newsfoto Publishing Company.

Seekee, Vanessa. *Horn Island, In Their Steps 1939-45*. Riverwood, NSW: Ligare Pty. Ltd., 2002.

Taggart, William C. & Cross, Christopher. *My Fighting Congregation*. Garden City, New York: Doubleday, Doran & Company, 1943.

Walker, Howell. *American Bombers Attacking from Australia*. Washington, DC: National Geographic Society, January 1943.

Waters, Damian. *Beau's, Butchers, & Boomerangs-Mareeba*. Brisbane, Queensland Australia: Watson Ferguson & Company, 2003.

White, W. L. *Queens Die Proudly*. New York: Harcourt, Brace and Company, 1943.

Willmott, H. P. *B-17 Flying Fortress*. Secaucus, New Jersey: Chartwell Books, 1980.

Magazines and Newspapers

Time Magazine. "Last Parade"; February 22, 1943.

Rattlesnake Bomber Base Magazine. Public Relations Office Army Air Base: Published by University Supply and Equipment Co. Fort Worth, Texas; 1943.

Call, Tomme, ed. *The Rattler.* Pyote (TX) Pyote Army Airfield Public Relations Office: October 27, 1943. cover; p.4.

Koops, Pfc. E.C., ed. *The Rattler.* Pyote (TX) Pyote Army Airfield Public Relations Office: April 26, 1945.

La Junta Daily Tribune, December 1, 1942; January 12, 1943.

"Medal Presentations." Rattlesnake Bomber Base, *The Rattler*, CD-ROM. Hearst Metrotone, News, Oct, 1943.

Koshare Indians. Explorer Post 2230, La Junta, Colorado. 1951.

19th Bomb Group History, WWI-WWII-Korea, Philippines, Java, Guam, CD-ROM. Landau

"Sgt. Elder Tells of Battles over South China Sea" *La Junta Daily Tribune*, January 12, 1943.

Hank Stratton, "Gunner returns to 1942 crash site," *Clarion News;* September 25, 1997.

Papers

Ferrell, Bud, "The 19th Bomb Group."

McAuliffe, Lt. Harold C. and DeShazo, Lt. Alexander D. "The

Bibliography

30th Squadron," Pyote, Texas, February 1943.

Summary Table: Planes destroyed in Philippines, 1941; Planes destroyed in Java, 1942; Planes destroyed in/ operating Australia, 1942. By Colonel Frank Cappelletti USAF, 19th BG veteran. Courtesy of Rose Cappelletti, wife of the Colonel.

Hicks, Betty, "Elder history and genealogy."

Interviews

Ralph Dietz with author, at Ralph's home in Clarion, Pennsylvania, October 3, 4, 2008.

Paul Eckley with author, telephone.

Elton Brown with author, telephone and at his home in Apache, Oklahoma, April, 2015.

Darrell Landau (Historian 19th Bomb Group); with author, week of October 21-26, 2010, Little Rock, Arkansas.

Lee Long with author, telephone.

Damian Waters, tour and description of Mareeba Air Base for Ken and Phyllis Bledsoe, Mareeba, Queensland Australia, September 25, 2010.

Vanessa Seekee, tour and description of 34th Australian Heavy Antiaircraft Battery sites on Horn Island, Sept, 27, 2010 including on site testimonials by Royal Australian Army Antiaircraft WWII veterans, Gordon Cameron and Gerry Merrett.

Correspondence

Appleton, Linda, to author, email, August 6. 2012.

Ashak, Sally A., to author, email, July 2, 2010.

Barber, Donita, to author, emails, March 28; April 7, 10, 14, 2014.

Bartsch, Bill, to author, emails, January 7, 9, 19, 22, 25, 28; February 15, 17, 2011. February 12, 24, 27, 2013.

Birdsall, Steve, to author, emails, March 31; April 1, 2010.

Brown, Elton, to author, emails, January 10, 20, 2011. January 7; June 4, 2012. July 28; August 11, 2013. October 7, 2014.

Buller, Mick, to author, emails, January 13, 2010. May 5, 2014.

Cappelletti, Rose, to author, emails, July 7, 10, 28, 29; August 14, 31, 2012. January 10, 11, 2015.

Cochran, Susan, Royal Gorge Regional Museum and History Center, to author, emails, October 26; November 2, 9, 2011.

Crowley County, Colorado Heritage Center, to author, email, January 26, 2009.

Dietz, Ralph, to author, emails, June 4, 10; October 20; November 28, 30; December 12, 2007. January 7, 28; February 4, 5; October 4; November 21, 2008. February 1; April 7; September 1, 2009.

Dunn, Peter, to author, emails, August 28, 2007. July 13, 2009. October 3, 2010.

Bibliography

Eckley, Paul, to author, emails, October 27, November 4, 17, December 1, 28, 2010; January 2, 6, March 4, August 19, 2011; June 11, 12, July 20, 21, 2012; February 4, 2013.

Falk, Dallas, to author, emails, February 14, June 25, August 8, 2014.

Farrell, Bud, to author, emails, June 27, 29, 30; July 10, 11, 2014.

Fuller, Craig, to author, email, June 1, 2007.

FOIA OFFICER, Department of the Army, to author, April 9, 2009.

Harvard University Archives Reference Staff, to author, email, October 1, 2014.

Johnson, Shirley, to author, March, 2010.

Larkin, Sandra, to author, email, April 3, 2009.

Lindsey, Dr. Keith, to author, September 5, 2014; May 31, June 1, 5, August 13, 2012.

Invited to and attended Lindsey family reunion, August 4, 2012. Lindsey, Larry, to author, emails, May 29, July 25, 2012.

Long, Lee, to author, emails, December 15, 21, 23, 24, 2011. February 9, 2012; January 14, August 4, 2013.

Maine, Tony, to author, email, December 22, 2014.

Marks, Roger, to author, email, August 18, 20, 2012.

Mathewson, T.D., to author, letter, January 18, 2014

Michael, Jerry, to author, email, August 15, 2006; January 10,

August 23, 2011.

Musumeci, Mick, to author, emails, January 11,13,16,19, 23, 25; February 7; March 16, 18, 19, 25, 27, 28. February 11, 14, 2012; November 20; December 3, 4, 7, 8, 11, 17, 2013; November 4, 5; December 19, 2014.

Napieralski, Joe, to author, email, January 12, 2013.

O'Bryan, Dr. Bob, to author, emails, August 21, 24, 31; September 13, 18, 19, 2011; October 4, 2012.

Olson, Janice, to author, email, March 31, 2006.

Paul, Diane, to author, email, March 24, 2010.

Polson, Virginia, to author, email, May 29, 31, 2012.

Porter, Bill, to author, email, May 28, 2009.

Prideaux, Maj. Mark, Royal Australian Army, emails, November 20, 24, 2010; May 10, 2012.

Quiggle, Bonnie, to author, e-mails, May 27, 28, 30, June 5, 7, 24, 2012.

Regalbuti Sr, John, to author, email, June 1, 8, 2009.

Richardson, Jane, to author, emails, April 5, 9, 18, 28, 29, May 2, 7, 9, 24, 28, September 30, October 31,November 2, 3, 5, 14, 19, December 26, 2009. January 15, 19, March 17, 18, 22, 23, June 13, October 17, 2010. August 2, 22, 2011. March 6, 2014.

Rodgers, Edward, to author, emails, January 27, 28, 30, February

Chapter 1: Foundation Built on Feathers

8,9,25, March 2, December 3, 6, 7, 14, 15, 2011. January 8, 18, 25, February 5, 2012. September 6, 23, 2014.

Seekee, Liberty and Vanessa, to author, emails, May 23, December 16, 2007; February 29, March 30, 2008. January 14, May 2, June 17, August 28, October 6, 15, 18, December 3, 2010; January 24, March 3, 10, 13, 29, 31, April 1, 6, 24, May 2, August 9, October 6, 11. 2011; May 23, 2012.

Spieth, Glen, to author, emails, September 16, 2007. January 4, 2008.

Taylan, Justin, to author, emails, February 1, 24, 2009.

Waters, Damian, to author, email, May 28, 29, June 4, October 18, November 9, 10, December 10, 2010; December 10, 2011.

Wingerd, Renee, to author, emails, April 2, 5, 7, 11, 21, 28, 2010; May 3, 7, 30, June 3, 2012.

Official Documents

War Department; Headquarters, Fifth Air Force, November 7, 1942. Letter sent by General George C. Kenney, Commanding General of Allied Air Forces in Southwest Pacific Area to Lerenna Elder. Decoration of Silver Star to Sgt. Vernon Elder for gallantry in action over Vunakanau Airdrome, Rabaul, New Britain.

HEADQUARTERS FIFTH AIR FORCE APO 923
16 January, 1943

General Orders # 11   Section I

OFFICIAL CREDIT FOR DESTRUCTION OF
ENEMY AIRCRAFT
ELDER, VERNON Sgt. 6291168 30th Bomb Squadron

Personal Materials

Black/white photos, 1941-42-43. California; Java; Cloncurry, Qld.; Mareeba, Qld.; Port Moresby, New Guinea; aerial on mission; at sea, *SS Torrens;* San Francisco harbor; 'Rattlesnake' Bomber Base, Pyote, Texas.

Summary account of 19th BG B-17 planes destroyed on the ground; Clark Field, 12-8-41 to 12-25-41; Planes destroyed in Java; 1-11-42 to 2-8-42; Planes destroyed in/operating Australia; 12-27-41 to 1-11-42, Lt. Frank Cappelletti, 30th BS, 19th BG.

DIARY and LETTERS HOME by Vernon Elder, Army Air Corps, 19th Bomb Group, 1941-42.

Date	Type	Location
Nov. 25, '41	letter	Fort McDowell, Angel Island, San Francisco
Nov. 28, '41	letter	Fort McDowell, Angel Island, San Francisco
Dec. 3, '41	letter	Fort McDowell, Angel Island, San Francisco
Dec. 4, '41	letter	San Francisco
Dec. 5, '41	diary	aboard *SS President Johnson*
Dec. 6, '41	diary	aboard *SS President Johnson*
Dec. 7, '41	diary	aboard *SS President Johnson*

Bibliography

Date	Type	Location
Dec. 8, '41	diary	aboard *SS President Johnson*
Dec. 8, '41	diary	aboard *SS President Johnson*
Dec. 9, '41	diary	aboard *SS President Johnson*
Dec. 10, '41	diary	San Francisco State Park
Dec. 10, '41	telegram	Fort Mason, California
Dec. 11, '41	diary	San Francisco State Park
Dec. 12, '41	letter	San Francisco
Dec. 15, '41	letter	March Field, California
Dec. 18, '41	letter	Bakersfield, California
Dec. 19, '41	log	Bakersfield, California
Dec. 22, '41	letter	Bakersfield, California
Dec. 25, '41	letter	McDill Field, Tampa, Florida (Beginning of Africa Route)
Dec. 29, '41	post card/log	Tampa, Florida
Dec. 30, '41	letter/log	Trinidad, Br. West Indies
Dec. 31, '41	log	Belem, Brazil
Jan. 3, '42	log	Accra
Jan. 4, '42	letter	Transit West Africa

Jan. 6, '42	log	Accra
Jan. 7, '42	log	Accra
Jan. 12, '42	log	Accra
Jan. 13, '42	log	Kano
Jan. 14, '42	log	Khartoum
Jan. 14, '42	letter	Khartoum Anglo Egyptian Sudan, Africa
Jan. 15, '42	log	Steamer Point Aden
Jan. 19, '42	log	Kirache, India
Jan. 20, '42	log	Bangalore, India
Jan. 21, '42	letter	<u>Censored</u>, India
Jan. 21, '42	log	Palembang, Sumatra
Jan. 22, '42	log	Surabaya, Java
Jan. 23, '42	log	arrived Malang 6 am
Jan. ?, '42	log	first mission
Jan. 30, '42	telegram	now in Malang, "impossible to write at present"

<u>NOTES</u>: *Vernon mailed letters home from February 1942 through April 1942. None of the letters were ever received by his mother until one written May 22, 1942.*

Notes and References

Chapter 1 Foundation Built on Feathers

1. Koshare Indians. Explorer Post 2230, La Junta, Colorado. 1951.
2. Elder letter written home, September 20, 1942.
3. John H. Mitchell, In Alis Vicimus, On Wings We Conquer, p. 17.
4. Tom Brokaw, The Greatest Generation, xix. 1998.
5. Elder letters, reaction to Pearl Harbor attack, December 11, 22, 1941.
6. Lt. Harold McAuliffe, Lt. Alexander DeShazo, "30th Squadron," February 1943.
7. Elder letters . . . impatience and uncertainty.
8. Homesickness.
9. Western Union Telegram from Vernon O. Elder, January 30, 1942.

Chapter 2 Every Squeak and Rattle

1. Darrell Landau, 19th Bomb Group Diary, January 26, 1942.
2. Lt. Col. Eugene T. Carson, Wing Ding, p. 55.
3. Landau.
4. Bud Ferrell, The 19th Bomb Group, p. 2.
5. James D. Rorrison, Nor the Years Contemn: Air War on the Australian Front 1941-42, p. 235.
6. William H. Bartsch, Every Day A Nightmare, p. 334.
7. Walter D. Edmonds, They Fought With What They Had, pp. 443-44.
8. Edward Jablonski, Flying Fortress, p. 65.
9. John H. Mitchell, p. 100.
10. Rorrison, (members of the 19th and 7th BG, USAAF) statement to the writer.
11. Ibid, p. 287.
12. Ibid, p. 287.
13. Landau, quote by Lt. L. H. May.
14. Gene Eric Salecker, Fortress Against the Sun, p. 172.
15. H. McAuliff, 19th Bomb Group Diary.
16. Bruce Gamble, Rabaul, p. 67.
17. Jablonski, p. 69.
18. Salecker, p. 210.
19. R. B. Gooch, 19th Bomb Group Diary.
20. Jablonski, p. 69.

21. Ibid, pp. 69-70.
22. Peter Nielsen, Diary of WWII North Queensland, p. 148.
23. Jablonski, p. 70.
24. Samuel Elliot Morison, The Two-Ocean War, p. 122.
25. Jablonski, p. 70.

Chapter 3   Somewhere, Someplace, Overseas

1. Elder letter, May 22, 1942.
2. Major William C. Teats, excerpt from Turn of the Tide found in the 19th Bomb Group Diary.
3. Bruce Gamble, p. 55.
4. Vern Haugland, The AAF Against Japan, p. 69.
5. Teats.
6. Priscilla Hardison, The Suzy-Q, p. 83.
7. Salecker, p. 212.
8. La Junta Daily Tribune, January 11, 1943.

Chapter 4   Mareeba

1. Damian Waters, Beau's, Butchers, & Boomerangs, p. 26.
2. Hardison, p. 83.
3. Howell Walker, National Geographic, January 1943, p. 68.
4. Steve Birdsall, Flying Buccaneers, pp. 24-25.
5. Hardison, pp. 125-26.
6. Waters, p. 33.
7. Elder letters, May 22; June 22, 26; July, 1942.
8. General George C. Kenney, General Kenney Reports, p. 42.

Chapter 5   Wounded Eagle

1. Vanessa Seekee, Horn Island, In Their Steps, p. 195.
2. USAAFDATA Personal Records and IDPF.
3. Elder letter, July 22, 1942.
4. Seekee, Lance Potter comment, p. 52.
5. Elder letter, July 22, 1942.
6. Schenectady Gazette, January 5, 1943, p. 3.
7. Salecker, pp. 129-30.
8. Dietz interview, October 3, 2007.
9. Seekee, Lance Potter comment, p. 198.
10. Elder letter to Otto Weiser, August 2, 1943.

Notes and References

11. Mick Buller, email to author, 2014.
12. Elder letter to Otto Weiser.
13. Elder letter, August 10, 1942.
14. Seekee, pp. 196-97.
15. Ibid, Major Rouse comment, pp. 198-99.
16. George Weller, Chicago Daily News, August 11, 1942.
17. Kenney, p. 59.
18. William C. Taggart, My Fighting Congregation, p. 152.
19. Charles P. Arnot, UP Correspondent, quote by Lt. Bob Wasson in Total War, Honolulu, June 8, 1943.
20. Doris Lindsey Darnell, Memories, 2001.
21. Elder letter, September 1, 1942.
22. Elder letter, October 4, 1942.
23. Elder letter, October 19, 1942.
24. Ibid.
25. Elder V-Mail, October 23, 1942.
26. Elder letter, November 21, 1942.
27. Letters written by Mrs. Fred Messmore and Mrs. Sue Crockett in July, August, and September, 1942.
28. Elder letter from Letterman Hospital, San Francisco, December 20, 1942.
29. Western Union Telegram from Presidio of San Francisco, December 29, 1942.

Chapter 6 'Rattlesnake' Bomber Base

1. Thomas E. Alexander, Rattlesnake Bomber Base, p. 87.
2. Ibid, p. 104.
3. Rattlesnake Bomber Base Magazine, 1943, p. 16.
4. Alexander, pp. 100-01.
5. Jablonski, p. 285.
6. Alexander, p. 156.
7. Ibid, p. 161.
8. Ibid, p. 162.
9. John W. Rice's letter to Sgt. Vernon Elder, September 11. 1943.

Chapter 7 Australian Connection

1. Peter Dunn, Australia at War website.
2. Seekee, p. 159.
3. Stratton, Clarion News, September 25, 1997.
4. Seekee, p. 197.

5. Cappelletti Summary of B-17s destroyed or operated in Australia during 1941-42.

Chapter 8 The Letter

1. Elder letter to Ottor Weiser.
2. Doris Mae's letter to John Rice, August 20, 1943.
3. Renee Wingerd, Rice Family History, p. 3.

Chapter 9 Adventure 'Down Under'

1. Bill Bryson, In A Sunburned Country, p. 6.
2. Waters, on back book cover.
3. Ibid.
4. 34th Heavy Antiaircraft Battery, Royal Australian Army.
5. Wikipedia.org., Torres Strait Islanders.
6. 51st Battalion, Far North Queensland Regiment, Royal Australian Army.

Chapter 10 Long Ago, But Not Forgotten

Summary

1. H. P. Willmott, B-17 Flying Fortress, 1980.

Epilogue

1. "Buddies Report Lindsey Killed on Flare Test," Canon City Daily Record.
2. Email from Rose Cappelletti, July 10, 2012.

Acknowledgments

I am greatly indebted to the following contributors who, each in their own way, provided information that ultimately led to our discovery and confirmation of my father's B-17 bomber site:

Vanessa and Liberty Seekee provided us with the best information known about the Army Air Corps' accidents in the Torres Strait as well as the location of B-17 #655.

Ralph Dietz, a survivor of the crash, whom we interviewed in Clarion, Pennsylvania in 2008. Ralph's account helped us understand the fears and actions of the crew after hitting the ocean.

Paul Eckley, co-pilot in the 93rd Squadron, who through our many phone conversations, described the ever present challenges of flying through violent tropical storms to bomb the well defended Japanese.

A special thanks to Shirley Johnson, Diane Paul, and Renee Wingerd, who through their many efforts led me to find my father's 'long lost letter' to Houston Rice's father describing the events off Horn Island that stormy night.

John Regalbuti Sr. provided a picture of Lt. Edward R. Budz, the navigator who died in the accident.

Bill Porter provided the only known picture of Sgt. James Houchins, the bombardier, also a casualty.

Edward Rogers provided primary documentation through newspaper sources describing the incident.

Susan Cochran of the Royal Gorge Regional Museum and History Center, provided many articles from local newspapers about Lt. Paul Lindsey's tragedy off Cairns, Australia.

Bonnie Quiggle provided the pictures of Lt. Lindsey's days at Colorado A&M and of him after his commission in the Army Air Corps.

Rose Cappelletti provided letters and pictures, including navigation maps, that her late husband, Col. Frank Cappelletti, had saved. The most important contribution to my research, however, was the record Frank kept documenting each B-17 destroyed or operated in Australia during the time the 19th BG was there. His account of #636 and #655 validated Vernon's and Ralph's stories of the location of these two crashes.

Dr. Bob O'Bryan, my high school classmate, provided pictures of 19th Bomb Group pilots, one of whom was his father, Lt. Carey O'Bryan, Jr.

My cousin, Betty Hicks, provided pictures of the Elder family, especially, of my father during his early years.

An Australian friend and historian, Mick Musemeci, provided a picture of my father, Sgt. Vernon Elder, standing next to his tail gunner position while in Mareeba, Australia in 1942. This is the picture that was ultimately chosen to appear on the cover of this book. Good on ya' mate!

Teresa Funke provided a road map for us to follow while navigating the world of writing and publishing a book.

Matt Hehn rescued me from the ever changing complexities of today's computers.

There would have been no story had Vernon's letters not been saved by Grandmother Elder over seventy years ago. As my wife, Phyllis, meticulously arranged them in chronological order in 2005, Vernon's story and our adventure began to take shape

Finally, I must thank my wife and stepfather, Bill Bledsoe, for their encouragement and support during my work on this extended project. Without their interest, I may not have found the courage and determination to overcome the road blocks every researcher must face in order to 'tell the story.'

About the Author:

Ken Elder Bledsoe was raised in New Mexico but has lived in Colorado most of his life. He is a graduate of Fort Lewis College with a degree in history and a master's degree from Colorado State University. He served six years in both the New Mexico and Colorado Army National Guard and was cited for "exceptional service in providing emergency medical treatment to victims of an auto accident" and presented the Meritorious Service Medal. After 33 years as an award winning social studies teacher, he retired. When he was four, Bledsoe's parents divorced; and he had limited contact with his father, Vernon O. Elder, a WWII Pacific War veteran. Vernon was a tail gunner on a B-17 Flying Fortress with the 19th Bombardment Group and had many harrowing experiences that he and Ken never had a chance to discuss. In an effort to learn more about his father, Ken joined the 19th BG Association and has interviewed several men who served with Vernon. His quest to know led him half way around the world. Writing this book has instilled in Ken much pride and admiration for Vernon – both as a warrior and as a man. Ken lives in Fort Collins, Colorado.

email: kpbledsoe@comcast.net

Made in the USA
San Bernardino, CA
05 May 2017